UNSE
FOOTPR
S H E R I D A N   V O Y S E Y

Your path led through
the sea... though your
footprints were not seen.

ANCIENT HEBREW SONG

A Lion Book
an imprint of
Lion Hudson plc
Wilkinson House, Jordan Hill Road
Oxford, OX2 8DR, England
www.lionhudson.com

ISBN 978 0 7459 5293 2 (UK)
ISBN 978 0 8254 6188 0 (USA)

This book was originally printed by Scripture Union Australia in 2005.
Scripture Union Australia
Locked Bag 2
Central Coast Business Centre
NSW 2252, Australia
www.scriptureunion.org.au

First Lion edition 2007
10 9 8 7 6 5 4 3 2 1 0

A catalogue record for this book is available from the British Library

Cover art and internal design by Nicole Gillan.
Printed and bound in Malta

The text paper used in this book has been made from wood
independently certified as having come from sustainable forests.

FOREWORD

On a recent birthday, my father-in-law was opening some presents with the help of his granddaughter. As the eager two-year-old helped tear away the wrapping from a square-shaped object, she excitedly said, "Oh, it's a book!" When they opened the book, however, the child's excitement turned sour. "Aww," she sighed, "it's got words."

Sometimes a new book can bring the same response from adults. Arriving home with our purchase we hit the couch and open the cover with anticipation of some new story, insight, or imaginary destination. But instead all we find is words – symbols strung together with little to ignite the heart.

I hope this book is not like that for you. Instead, I hope *Unseen Footprints* is something of a reflective journey that helps open your eyes to realities that lie present before you; realities that really can enflame the heart.

A number of people have helped shape the thoughts within these pages. Among them are Peter Baade, Alison Brandon, Allen Browne, Jason and Belinda Gor, and Tony and Vivienne Voysey – all of whom gave vital feedback on numerous drafts of the book. Working with Sally Smith's editorial expertise has been a delight, and Nicole Gillan's design skills have allowed the book to speak through image and space as much as word and sentence. I am so thankful for this team.

And I should apologize in advance for my language in relation to God, as some may not like it. My journey has led me to believe that the divine being is more than an impersonal energy, and so I couldn't use "it" as a description with integrity. And while I believe God is beyond gender, using variants of "s/he" felt awkward. So I often describe God as "he" which has also enabled me to quote the wisdom of others past and present without alteration.

Finally, *Unseen Footprints* is dedicated to my wife Merryn, a woman who helps me discern God's unseen footprints, and without whom I could never accomplish projects like this.

I hope you enjoy the journey!

Sheridan Voysey

August 2005

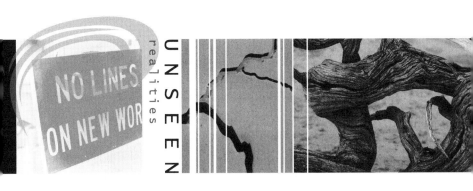

INTRODUCTION

In one vast and lonely desert lies a secret.

As winds sweep along the parched soil of the land – kicking particles of dust into the air, tousling the spikey Spinifex grass, ruffling the fur of the few animals scavenging for moisture – an unseen reality lies beneath its surface:

Water.

Trillions of litres of water.

Around five years ago an underground basin was found in Western Australia's Great Victoria desert. Beneath the red sand, sticks and scrub of that desolate land lay a reservoir holding a potential two trillion kilolitres of slightly saline water. In Perth, the state's capital city, the media compared the find to one of its well-known dams, the Mundaring Weir. The basin's capacity was equivalent to 31,000 Mundaring Weirs. That arid desert may have looked like death from above, but underneath flowed a river of life.

A giant lake in the desert – what an unexpected surprise. Stories like that remind me that "unseen" does not equal "unreal". I wonder how many trekked across that dusty land oblivious of the life beneath them. I wonder how many still do.

I also wonder how many unseen realities lie beneath the surface of our lives. Most of us have days when we sense a world of vivid colour is out there, but remains shrouded from us. Instead of seeing bright reds and purples we see only pastels. But through a brush with serendipity – the unexpected surprise – the veil lifts for a moment and we glimpse the vibrancy of that other world. And in that moment we sense something bigger than us has been encountered. Perhaps *Someone* bigger than us.

What if coincidences weren't so coincidental?

What if serendipitous experiences had been "arranged" just for us?

What if unseen footprints walked before us, behind us and beside us?

An ancient Hebrew song picks up on such ideas. "Your path led through the sea," it poetically records, "though your footprints were not seen." The song reflects the experiences of a community thousands of years ago who had encountered an unseen reality. They had followed this presence and been lead out of their raging sea of troubles. While their eyes hadn't seen it in the material sense, this community knew that they had encountered the divine.

This book, *Unseen Footprints*, is about opening our spiritual eyes to see the activities of the divine around us. Could life flow right beneath our noses, just like that desert discovery? Could we have had encounters with the divine that we haven't yet recognised as such? Could God be written into the drama of our lives as if played by a secondary character or an extra that we haven't paid much attention to?

I think so.

Faith is to believe what we do not see, and the reward of faith is to see what we believe.

AUGUSTINE

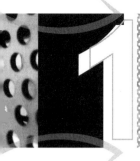

>>> **CHAPTER ONE**

PAIN: THE
JOURNEY BEGINS

The eccentric figure stares back at me from the newspaper clipping.

He is centre frame with Dasher, his former harness racer, standing placidly by his left side. Behind him rests a hand-built cart – standard car wheels, a steel chassis, tin sheet walls and roof, canvas roll up doors and an upturned gumboot balanced on one of its thin crossbraces. This two-metre-long cart is this nomad's home, a space just long enough to stretch his swag out at night and just wide enough to allow Rowdy the dog protection during rainy evenings.

For nearly a decade now Bill has trotted around Australia on this horse and cart, writing poetry, chatting to Rowdy. A child of the bombed generation, his earliest memories shattered by World War II, at the age of sixty Bill harnessed Dashing Romeo (shortened to Dasher to prevent delusions of grandeur) and set out on his solitary journey. Ever since, Bill's been wandering through life, happy to be a self-confessed "runaway grandfather". He is amazed at the assistance he receives along the nation's dusty and often uninhabited outback trails and highways.

People buy his groceries and return with change, others offer to do his washing and it arrives the following day, clean and delivered by someone travelling in the opposite direction. Bill is happy to be the object of fellow travellers' curiosity and has no plans of stopping anywhere for good just yet. These days his ultimate ambition is simply to make it to the next waterhole.

A wandering soul who trades the career path for wide open roads, relational angst for solitude, suburban banality for a rickshaw cart and a writing pad. I find Bill's journey intriguing, and symbolic of the inner restlessness many of us feel.

The desire to escape.

To seek.

To ditch life and set out on a new unknown pathway, aided by the kindness of strangers.

A little voice inside us whispers, there's got to be more to existence than painful childhood memories, office competition for the next promotion, the mundaneness of grocery shopping and the predictability of Monday morning back at work.

I don't think there's one person
who has ever lived who didn't
say, "This isn't working. I need
something else".

AUTHOR, DOUGLAS COUPLAND[1]

[aching hearts]

Sitting on my desk in front of me is a stack of newspaper clippings, photocopied articles and printouts from internet sites – an inch-high mound of stories like Bill's describing the journeys of those seeking more from the adventure of life. In addition, I've had the privilege of spending numerous hours conducting interviews with people seeking meaning. While many of these travellers have taken different pathways in their search for "something more", there arises one common theme between them:

Pain.

- A teenage girl is attracted to Wicca because of its promise of self-empowerment and control over life's events.

- A suburban mother of four discovers that meditation helps her overcome the stress of her relationships. She is about to go on her second silent retreat – where she won't speak a word or see anyone for three months.

- Maureen, a grandmother, is diagnosed with cancer and given two years to live. She now attends psychic development classes to help her make sense of it all.

- Paul, 31, had a drug addiction and a failing business when he began searching for answers by consulting spirit guides.

- Martin couldn't cope after his relationship breakdown, and now spends hundreds of dollars each month for the advice of his "personal coach".

- A popular radio broadcaster is listened to by thousands but can't form meaningful, intimate friendships. Her loneliness drives her to seek answers and she begins attending church.

- A businesswoman can't get over the grief of losing her sister in a car accident. In the past few months she has spent nearly $15,000 attending the seminars of a popular New Age guru.

- A sexuality columnist has an emotional breakdown and pursues healing through a more spiritual approach to life. She now helps others discover the path to peace and the "god within".

The stories could continue – one person after another who has tasted suffering and set out on a journey to overcome it, transform it, or simply make sense of it. For these people pain is still an unwelcome intruder, yet it has spurred them on to explore the greater, more substantive issues of life, meaning and the world of the spirit. Perhaps pain reminds us that we're not fully in control; that in fact we are finite, and not the limitless beings we believed we were as kids leaping from the fence, hoping to fly.

When we're brought up as kids they try and make us think we're in control. You know that's stupid really.

We're on a planet hurtling at 108,000 kilometres per hour through space, and rotating at 1700 kilometres per hour. And here's a little human on earth saying, "I'm in control, I'm in control." That is stupid.

LANDSCAPE PHOTOGRAPHER, KEN DUNCAN

[dissatisfied souls]

Pain often launches our search for something more. But this pain may not be the physical or even emotional kind, but the ache of an empty soul. For many, our spirit is no longer satisfied with long-held dreams becoming actualized. We can experience boardroom success, bedroom bliss, and pursue dollars and desires and experiences and highs. But a deeper rumbling is felt below the surface of the self, a hollow void in one's core despite such achievements.

Back to that pile of clippings on my desk:

- The author of a globally popular book wonders why his success doesn't satisfy his longing for significance.

- A mid-forties woman wanders around the mind-body-spirit festival in her city, yet is still searching for the book, seminar or experience that will 'click' with her.

- A twenty-something man joins a psychic tour of the United Kingdom hoping the experience will provide some kind of answers to life and the nature of the unseen world.

- A university student reflects on the seeming futility of life. After her degree, work. After work, perhaps children. After children, perhaps a return to work, and after that, old age and death. The same fate befell her parents, awaits her friends, and is in store for the children she will bear. She wonders if there's any purpose to her existence beyond this cycle of work-sleep-struggle-die.

Perhaps you've felt something similar. Encountering the greatest of life's offerings – human intimacy, career progress, maybe even bungee jumping from the wall of Switzerland's Verzasca Dam (all 220 metres of it) – these experiences feel good, but there is still a chamber within that echoes with questions:

Why doesn't this thrill last?

Why am I never completely satisfied?

(Why does my back hurt after that bungee jump?)

A world free of pain – in body, mind and soul – is every human's ultimate hope. It is the prayer of every child; the wish that makes shopping centre Santas stumble for an adequate reply as little wide-eyed faces stare hopefully up from their knees. No one in their right mind would choose a life, a world, a universe where pain is present.

Yet, on a globe that coexists with war, death and lymphoma, pain can serve a purpose. Pain grips us by the shoulders, looks us straight in the eye and screams, "you cannot ignore me! You must deal with the questions I am raising." And so for many, pain is the catalyst for a searching that takes them on a journey to places they'd never originally imagined, pathways they never would have ventured down and stopping points they would be the poorer without having visited.

There is no problem
so big it cannot be run
away from.

PEANUTS CARTOON : CHARLES M. SCHULZ

This, of course, assumes that we face our pain. The reality is, most of us want to run from it. We leave the troubling fiancé, move across the country to avoid business debts, overwhelm bad memories with stimulants, fill the emptiness with another shopping trip.

Perhaps even hitch our cart to a horse and become a runaway grandfather.

Yet, the world's greatest treasures, masterpieces and breakthroughs are birthed when someone stares back into the face of pain, submits to its interrogation and addresses its desperate questions. Is a cure for cancer possible? they ask. Can my marriage be saved? How can we feed starving children in Uganda? Is there an afterlife? Can I beat this depression? Is my soul longing for something that will last? We have developed anaesthetic, eradicated smallpox, increased global literacy rates, decreased poverty and increased life expectancy in the last century, all because someone faced pain and pursued its questions.

Aching in body, heart or soul? A journey of the spirit beckons.

Perhaps the English author CS Lewis was right when he suggested that "God whispers to us in our pleasure, speaks to us in our conscience, but shouts to us in our pain; it is his megaphone to rouse a deaf world." A life that finds meaning, purpose and beauty, a life that aids others and encounters the divine, is a life discovered in the midst of pain not in its absence. And as my pile of newspaper cuttings and interview stories tells me, those who begin the search to encounter the divine along the journey of life do so because they have stared pain in the face and yearned for something more.

>>> **CHAPTER TWO**

YEARNING:
THE JOURNEY
INTENSIFIES

It was late and the nightclub was packed.

I was one of the four featured DJs for the event – a dance party showcasing some of the hottest club music around, played by some of my city's (supposedly) best disc jockey talent. Of the four of us headlining that evening, one would go on to international success as a dance music DJ and record producer, another would become a member of one of Australia's most successful urban music outfits, and the third was a smooth turntablist with extensive acclaim amongst the city's clubbing fraternity.

And then there was me.

Nightclubs, dreams & positive thinking

I had been awakened to the creative possibilities of record mixing from the age of twelve when I first saw the film *Beat Street*. A poorly scripted flick with little plot but a heaping helping of New York street culture, *Beat Street* displayed what a DJ could do with two turntables – mixing records with similar tempos into a seamless party soundtrack. Somehow I wanted to learn how to be so clever and creative with music. When I grew up, I decided, I was going to be a nightclub DJ.

As a teenager I experimented with all manner of dilapidated equipment, hooking multiple tape decks and barely-useable record players together, trying to hone my skills with songs taped off the radio and the occasional twelve-inch record bought with pocket money. By the time I was sixteen I felt my time had come. All I needed to succeed as a DJ was a chance.

So, I called a city nightclub (the brazenness scares me now) and actually arranged a face-to-face chat with its manager. The manager overlooked my naivety and arranged for me to meet their house DJ by returning that evening. Return I did and before long I was looking after the decks most Saturday nights while the employed jock enjoyed free drinks at the bar. (Oh, they never knew about my underage status.)

A few years later I had achieved runner-up in a state-wide DJ mixing competition. And that win was why I was now standing in this nightclub, facing hundreds of people ready to hear me do my stuff.

But that evening I was mildly aware that something wasn't adding up. I was starting to realize my dreams, achieving in competitions and getting my name printed on posters and hand bills. Sure, in the grand scheme of things my success was minor – I wasn't even well known in my city's clubbing scene yet, let alone near achieving the international stardom of DJs like Carl Cox or Pete Tong. But shouldn't I be feeling better than this?

The higher I climbed the ladder of my dreams the more restless I seemed to feel.

The more success I achieved the more meaningless life seemed to be.

It didn't make sense.

Something within me yearned for something more.

[Fame] was touted as something that would raise your self-esteem and provide you with eternal happiness. Food would taste better, people would be more exciting, relationships would be great... I wish people could achieve what they think would give them happiness in order for them to realise that's not the way happiness can be found.

SINGER-SONGWRITER, ALANIS MORRISETTE[1]

As I surveyed the people around me that evening in the nightclub, I felt lonely. This life seemed to be working for them. Why wasn't it for me?

In reality I wasn't alone with such feelings. Sometimes you get to see a dream realized and discover the dream wasn't that great to begin with. As the party ends and the streamers are swept up, you realise you yearn for something greater, deeper, more lasting. Within us all lie longings that simple success, affirmation and wealth fail to meet. Pain may launch our journey towards "something more", but this deeper yearning intensifies it.

What kind of yearnings are we talking about?

There's tremendous yearning out there. There are a lot of people on a variety of spiritual walks. Those in their twenties are really starting to see that the materialistic-only lifestyle is a fairly hollow old shell.

PETER GARRETT[2]

[yearning for purpose]

I loved Sofia Coppola's movie *Lost in Translation*. Bob Harris
(played by Bill Murray) and Charlotte (Scarlett Johansson)
are two Americans visiting Tokyo. Bob, an aging film star,
has been brought in to shoot a whisky commercial for a
Japanese distillery, while the bored Charlotte gazes out her
hotel window having accompanied her husband to the city
on a work assignment. Suffering insomnia, Bob and Charlotte
wander down to the hotel bar late one night and cross paths.
Their chance meeting develops into a surprising friendship.

Despite their differences in age, gender and most other
things, Bob and Charlotte are drawn together by the one
thing they share – a disorientation in life. Bob is living off
his fading fame, unsure of what his future holds. Charlotte
has a Philosophy degree but doesn't know where her life
is heading. Bob's marriage is in trouble with phone calls to
his wife reduced to arguments about carpet colours for their
home renovation. Charlotte's two-year union with her trendy
photographer husband is marred by his workaholism. (In
a telling scene, the husband sits on the floor of their hotel
bedroom arranging his camera equipment. There is not
a flicker of distraction as Charlotte walks past him in her
underwear.)

Finding themselves in a city whose language they do not
know, with marriages they can't make work and futures
they can't foresee, Bob and Charlotte drift through Tokyo's
streets, restaurants and karaoke bars engaged in a search for
meaning. In one of my favourite scenes, Charlotte ambles
through an amusement centre staring blankly at the people
around her engrossed in their arcade games. The lights
flash, the laser effects whiz and zap, but she remains the cool
observer, disconnected from a world seemingly amusing itself
to death.

Although I am a woman and an artist and a female and a singer and a mother and a this and a that, still who am I? It's the question. It's the basic philosophical, spiritual question. What am I? What am I doing here? And it's still there for me.

SINGER-SONGWRITER, ANNIE LENNOX[3]

Lost in Translation is well written, subtly acted and full of humour and atmosphere. But to me the film's greatest quality is its portrayal of lost-ness – that sense of disorientation most humans feel at some time in their lives; that drive to discover our purpose for breathing and the resulting disconnection experienced when answers elude us.

Because in the quiet moments – perhaps as we lie waiting for sleep and we reflect on the day's successes and failures, in the solitude where the distractions of life and work can't reach us – we hear a murmur, a question that only in our bravest moments will we attend to:

So what?

So what about the money. So what about the home loan, or the holiday, or the dinner party. In the end what's life all about and what's my role within it?

[yearning for guidance]

In *Don Lane Show* a staple of Australian variety television
during the seventies and eighties, one of its segments proved
particularly popular. Each week Don and his team would
interview a classroom of children, asking them about their
aspirations, their joys and interests, who the most beautiful
person in the world was, and (of course) where babies came
from. The answers were cute and telling.

When SBS television recently revisited those segments I was
riveted. The producers chased down some of those original
five-year-olds to see what they'd made of their lives. All had
just turned thirty and the comparison between the five and
the thirty year old person was both touching and insightful.

Each interviewee was coping with adulthood in a different
way. One girl was single and wanted to be married. One
was a mother and feeling very content. Another had found
turning thirty a time of crisis since she hadn't met all the
goals she'd imagined herself reaching by that age. One of the
guys remarked that he'd only just begun to understand what
he liked and didn't in terms of hobbies, food and recreation.

Two of the original five-year-olds couldn't be part of the
programme. One had died in a car crash at the age of twenty-
seven. Seeing the original childhood footage alongside the
still photo of the grown man was saddening.

But my feelings were most intense for Julius, who even at the
age of five had found it difficult to fit in at kindergarten.

Who took a shine to playing the flute.

Who later developed depression.

Then schizophrenia.

And who later took his life after just twenty-five years on this planet.

Julius' mother was interviewed in his place for the programme. Her pain, loss, quivering lips and tear-streaked face were still with me as I lay in bed after the show that night.

I awoke the following morning and reflected on how fragile life is. Some dreams work out, and some don't. Some people struggle to fit into society while others seem to be given a red carpet entry. If life is a highway (as Tom Cochran sang), some are enjoying the drive in their BMW convertible while others are on the side of the road with their head under the bonnet. Life is tough, enjoyable, rewarding and heartbreaking – you never know what's around the corner.

And that is why we yearn for guidance.

Life, as the Danish philosopher Soren Kierkegaard mused, can only be understood backwards yet must be lived forwards. It would be so much easier if we could look back from the journey's end and make our decisions from that vantage point. But we can't. And with the uncertainty of the path ahead, it isn't unreasonable to cry out for direction now and then. Where will this path lead me? Will it end in regret?

Where am I going and which step should I take next?

For those moments when we'd like to be more certain than surprised by life, a number of divination options are available. Dream analysis has become a popular pastime if the bookstore shelves are anything to go by. Palm and tarot card readers are kept busy at market stalls. Seekers of guidance around the world read their horoscopes daily, hoping today's planetary positions will put them in a positive place for starting a relationship or changing careers. But whose guidance is reliable; which voices can we trust?

A couple of years ago Britain's biggest-selling hiking magazine apologised to its readers after publishing a trail that would lead climbers off the edge of a cliff. The magazine concerned gave advice on how to make a safe descent from Scotland's Ben Nevis mountain during bad weather. But during the editing process the first of two crucial bearings was inadvertently deleted. Instead of providing guidance on a safe descent, the magazine's directions would actually lead readers off the north face of the 1,344-metre mountain! I wouldn't have liked to have been the person responsible. Ben Nevis is notorious for its changeable weather and has claimed the lives of several climbers in the past.

Even the wisest human guides can lead us down the wrong path sometimes. Which makes our yearning for guidance all the more intense.

In every human being is a deep, ongoing search for meaning and transcendence – part of the image of God in our very nature. Even if we flee God, the religious imprint remains… Everyone believes in some kind of deity – even if that deity is an impersonal substance such as matter, energy or nature.

AUTHOR, CHARLES COLSON[4]

[yearning for liberation]

In his novel *Memoirs of a Geisha*, Arthur Golden tells the story of Chiyo, a girl from an impoverished fishing village who grows up to become Sayuri, one of Japan's most celebrated entertainers. But her metamorphosis is anything but romantic.

Chiyo is only nine when she is sold to a stranger by her father. Chiyo's unusual beauty lands her an apprenticeship in one of Kyoto's best-known okiya, or geisha houses, where she is renamed Sayuri and put to work doing menial labour about the home. The environment is loveless and made unbearable by head geisha Hatsumomo who becomes jealous of Sayuri's beauty. Hatsumomo manipulates circumstances and spreads lies about Sayuri which threaten to sink the apprentice's career before it begins. Luckily, a deal is struck between the okiya's manager and Mameha, one of Kyoto's most celebrated geisha, and Sayuri becomes Mameha's pupil.

Sayuri believes her survival lies in becoming a geisha like Mameha. She immerses herself in geisha education, learns the art of tea ceremonies and traditional dance, and learns how to play the shamisen. She entertains in Kyoto's most elegant tea houses, all the while fearing that her life may never be more than toil-filled struggle. Even Mameha dampens Sayuri's hopes. "We don't become geisha so our lives will be satisfying," she once says. "We become geisha because we have no other choice... Hopes are like hair ornaments. Girls want to wear too many of them, but when they become old, they look silly wearing even one."

Feeling hopeless in her situation, Sayuri is leaning by a stone wall weeping one afternoon when a man addresses her.

"Why, it's too pretty a day to be so unhappy."

Men would ordinarily ignore a girl like Sayuri, especially one crying. This man had not just bothered to speak, however, but had spoken to Sayuri kindly as if she were the daughter of a good friend. "For a flicker of a moment," she recollects, "I imagined a world completely different from the one I'd always known, a world in which I was treated with fairness, even kindness – a world in which fathers didn't sell their daughters." The Chairman takes out a handkerchief, wipes Sayuri's face, wraps a coin in the cloth and encourages her to buy some flavoured ice from a nearby vendor.

"In that brief encounter with the Chairman," Sayuri reflects, "I had changed from a lost girl facing a lifetime of emptiness to a girl with purpose in her life. Perhaps it seems odd that a casual meeting on the street could have brought about such change. But sometimes life is like that, isn't it?"

I love the wonder Arthur Golden has woven into his main character. As the Chairman walked away, Sayuri was still in her predicament. She was still a maid, was still pursuing a vocation she didn't really want, was still coming to terms with her father's betrayal. But somehow Sayuri had been awakened to a kindness that could touch the yearnings of her heart; a kindness that might bring hope and purpose where only the effects of cruelty had been known.

Each of us longs for liberation – to be freed from our pain, our past, the decisions we've made or the abuse we've encountered. Even the most fortunate recognise that this planet is groaning, that instead of running our race freely at times it feels like we're wading through molasses.

One problem is overcome when another is encountered. Just when the finances are getting back in shape, we lose our job and the carburettor packs in. A friend contracts cancer, our exaggerated tax return is found out, a businessman runs to the Caribbean with our investment.

Our suffering, fear and shame hint to us that we were never built for a world like this. Something's gone wrong and we long for liberation.

[yearning to belong]

"The biggest disease today," Mother Teresa of Calcutta once reminded us, "is not leprosy or tuberculosis, but rather the feeling of being unwanted, uncared for, and deserted by everybody." In addition to needing meaning, guidance and liberation, the human soul longs to belong – to experience a sense of home, security and relational warmth. From the street worker to the corporate mogul, each of us wonders if we are really special to anyone. That yearning to belong has led some into the most unexpected of destinies.

Donning the White Sheet

"I was five years old the first time I saw a black man," says Johnny Lee Clary in his thick Tulsa, Oklahoma drawl, "and I was amazed because I thought everybody was of white skin. Seeing a man with dark skin I turned to my father and said, 'look daddy, there's a chocolate-covered man'. But my dad replied, 'Son, that is not a chocolate-covered man. That is a nigger.' When my dad said that word he planted the seed of hate inside that five year old boy's heart."

And so begins the story of a boy who would later grow up to become the worldwide leader of the Ku Klux Klan. For seventeen years Johnny Lee Clary would taunt black people, burn down their churches and harrass their family members. But it was more than racism that attracted a young boy into one of the world's most hate-driven groups.

"When I was eleven," Johnny explains, "my father committed suicide in front of me. My mother had left him for another man. She was an alcoholic, a very sick woman, and she couldn't stand the sight of me because I reminded her too much of my daddy. She moved her new boyfriend into my father's house and told me to get out right after the funeral. I was sent to live in East Los Angeles with my sister.

My sister and her boyfriend were drug dealers and only tolerated me. She was only eighteen while her boyfriend was about forty. He had just gotten out of prison at the time, and he hated racists because he had drug clientele of all different colours of people. So when I said anything racist his solution to cure me of it was to beat me. I'd try to fight him back but I realised I wasn't a match for some old guy of forty. So, I just stayed out of his way and hung out on the streets. And I found myself trying to fit in with older kids.

"Teachers told me I was dumb, stupid, ignorant," Johnny remembers, "that I was a hoodlum and was going to end up in jail. They said it was a waste of their time trying to give me an education. So, I didn't feel like anyone cared about me.

"Then one day I saw David Duke, the leader of the Ku Klux Klan, interviewed on television. I wrote him for information. He wrote me back and sent all this literature. And then he sent an older man around to visit me. This man told me that I was smart, intelligent, that I needed a family and that I needed someone who would care about me. He told me the KKK would accept me and be a family to me."

Words like that hit their mark on a fourteen year old searching for acceptance. Johnny joined the KKK family.

Johnny started in the Klan's Youth Core, purchasing all the Klan literature he could get a hold of, memorising Klan bylaws and returning to Oklahoma where he began setting up new chapters. From this initiation Johnny's rapid ascent through Klan corporate ranks began. He became a bodyguard to David Duke at the age of eighteen and a state public relations rep by nineteen. At just twenty years of age he was the Grand Dragon for the state of Oklahoma. Finally, towards the end of his seventeen-year career, Johnny was unanimously voted in by his colleagues as the Imperial

Wizard of the Ku Klux Klan – the organization's highest office. Now he had the power, recognition and belonging he desired.

Johnny's tale portrays our deep need to meaningfully connect with a tribe. To him, even a racist, hate-riddled 'family' looked attractive. "At that point in time," Johnny says, "it could've been the Charles Manson family or Jim Jones' People's Temple. It could have been any other organization that told me I would be wanted, loved, accepted and part of a family – and I would have gone with them." Even when questions arose about the actions and integrity of the group, Johnny would always wipe them away with one thought:

"The Klan was there for me when no one else was."

A woman wanders Tokyo's streets looking for her purpose, an apprentice geisha yearns to be freed from her torments, a teenager in LA's concrete jungle longs to belong... yearnings these are for sure. But could they be signs of something more?

Why are such yearnings there, and why are they a universal experience?

Are they prompts that another world exists, that another reality awaits to be embraced? (Or for us to be embraced by?)

Creatures are not born with desires
unless satisfaction for those desires
exists. A baby feels hunger: well, there
is such a thing as food. A duckling
wants to swim: well, there is such a
thing as water… If I find in myself
a desire which no experience in this
world can satisfy, the most probable
explanation is that I was made for
another world.

AUTHOR, CS LEWIS[5]

[a turning point]

A yearning for "something more" was murmuring within my soul that May evening as I stood before that nightclub crowd. Purpose, guidance, belonging – I felt a vacuum for each even if I didn't have the vocabulary yet to express them. And soon I'd need liberation!

My DJ set that evening didn't go well. As if prey to some unseen cosmic forces, the moment I stepped up to the turntables the pair of headphones we were using stopped working. A bead of perspiration broke on my forehead as the club air conditioning froze the rest of my body. If I couldn't cue properly I couldn't mix properly. Dancers would have no idea of my plight but hear the full effect of its results. I could feel humiliation approaching.

As the current song edged towards its end we got a little sound through the headphones. I stumbled through my hour-long set with barely enough headphone volume to mix properly. Attempts at some of my well-planned tricks mostly failed. A second set of decks and equipment was arranged and the DJ following me proceeded to give the people what they had come for – a quality performance. I climbed down from the stage with my dreams in tatters and a deep emptiness like I'd never known. It sounds melodramatic but I vowed that night not to return to the club scene. And I didn't return. With no idea of what my alternative would be I walked out into the night air to head home.

Some years have past since the experience I have described. And now, looking back, I can see the outline of divine footprints on the stage from which I left humiliated. No, I don't think God was tinkering with the headphone wires. But I do think he was standing close by, whispering something to me:

That's right, Sheridan. You can't make this life work on your own. You were never meant to. Until you recognise that, the yearning will remain. But when you're ready, I'm here.

One must find God.
Marlene. Rome. Christmas.

LETTER FROM GERMAN ACTRESS MARLENE DIETRICH TO THE FRENCH SINGER EDITH PIAF

CHAPTER THREE

She was found crouching, her face against a rock, under an avalanche of sand.

When news came that a limestone cliff had collapsed, burying a group of children and adults on a West Australian beachfront, nearby beachgoers rallied with shovels and started desperately digging away the landslide. Most of those buried survived, but four children and five adults did not. Casualty numbers could have been one higher had it not been for the attention of one volunteer.

As rescuers worked frantically through dirt and rock, as spades dug fast and crow bars speared the wet, heavy sand to create air vents, a small voice was heard. "It was a very faint voice," said the local primary school cleaner who first heard the whisper. "You had to virtually bend down on the sand to hear it." The voice belonged to a ten-year-old girl who had been wedged between the falling sand and a large rock mass. With help from another rescuer the cleaner cleared away enough debris to reach through and grasp the girl's small hand. Fearing more rocks could collapse, sand and rock was patiently excavated from around the young life until, nearly one hour later, the girl was freed.

It pays to be attentive. It pays to listen. Surrounded by tragedy and danger one searcher listened closely, heard a whisper, and found life.

I see in this event a symbolic gesture of our search for the divine. Like this story of happy discovery in the midst of darkness, the divine can be found. But that discovery will only come to those who turn their curiosity into attentive listening, who incline their inner ear to detect the quiet voice, the whisper of God that beckons us. A whisper that leads us to life amidst the rubble of a groaning planet.

God was trying to get my attention that night in the nightclub. Could it be that the Creator wants more than our passing thought or occasional blasphemous reference when we've stubbed our toe, that he wants our attention, our ear – us? I think so. And so God whispers to us – perhaps many times throughout the course of each week:

- As we walk along the track of a mist-filled rainforest.

- Through the timely words of a friend.

- By a "coincidental" situation that saw us graciously benefited.

- Through our yearning, when we become aware that nothing in this life will fill the void within.

The utterances continue: heard as we enjoy a pleasurable meal, as the words of a song or book resonate with our predicament, while we're in the grip of a two-metre wave or are humbled by the might of a thunderstorm.

Some of these messages come as specific, individual

revelations while others are general signposts ready to be received when our eyes are open to them. No matter the form or timing, such whispers of divine interest carry a gentle persuasiveness, and are always personal.

What are these whispers and how can they be heard? It seems to me that a voice calls from behind the created world, from human desire and hope, through beauty and pleasure and other people, and occasionally even through direct address.

I have had a tremor of bliss,
a wink of heaven, a whisper.

TS ELIOT[1]

I am an agnostic, and all that means is that I really don't know. I assume there's a God because I can't figure out how anything, much less the whole universe, could have gotten here with no cause at all.

THE LATE COMIC, AUTHOR AND SINGER, STEVE ALLEN[2]

[a sublime world]

"If you're honest and you look at things around you,"
says landscape photographer Ken Duncan, "you realise
that there's a bigger thing going on than you. And it isn't
going on by accident. There is something behind it." It's
a sentiment most of us can identify with. As step follows
step along a rainforest path, as we stare down the plunging
fall of a Grand Canyon or experience the arid vastness of a
Nullarbor Plain, we feel a sense of awe. Confronted with the
sublime character of the created order it is not uncommon
to feel as if we are in the presence of something sacred. As
Elizabeth Barrett Browning so eloquently put it:

> *Earth is crammed with heaven*
> *And every bush aflame with God*
> *But only those who see take off their shoes.*[3]

Signs and Wonders

Ours is a most incredible universe – a cosmos of 50 billion known galaxies (the better the telescopes get, the more galaxies come into focus); a universe containing a revolving ball with conditions inexplicably hospitable to human life; a system of precise planetary motions producing consistent seasons on earth like clockwork.

For those who ponder, the world seems more like a gift from large and thoughtful hands than a cosmic illustration of random chance. Muse with me for a moment, and listen for a whisper:

- If our cosmos did begin with a big bang, it would have to have exploded with just the right amount of force for our universe to have formed. If it had burst with too little velocity the universe would have collapsed back in on itself shortly after the explosion. And if the blast had too much velocity matter would have streaked away so fast it would have been impossible for galaxies and solar systems to form.

- Earth is unique, lying just the right distance from the sun. If it were slightly closer all our water would boil away and life would be impossible. And if earth were only slightly further away from the sun all our water would freeze and our landscape would be nothing but barren deserts.

- Water itself has a host of unique properties indispensable for life. It is the only known substance whose solid phase, ice, is less dense than its liquid phase. If it were like normal substances ice would form on the bottom instead of the top of lakes, killing marine life below.[4]

- If gravity were only slightly stronger, stars would flame so fiercely they would burn out in a year leaving us with a universe of cinders. But if gravity were slightly weaker, stars couldn't form and the universe would be a thin undifferentiated blur. And had the force that binds atomic nuclei been only slightly weaker all atoms would disperse into vapour too.

- The chemical processes inside our bodies are designed to function within a narrow temperature range, and earth just happens to be exactly the right distance from the sun to fall within this range. For this to happen the earth must remain about the same distance from the sun at all times. Most planets have a distinctly elliptical orbit, but earth has a nearly circular orbit.

- Or consider the human body itself. When a pressurized blood circulation system is punctured, a clot must form quickly or the human or animal will bleed to death. But if blood congeals at the wrong time or place then the clot may block circulation, as it does with heart attacks and strokes. Mysteriously, blood knows just when and where not to clot. Also, a clot has to stop bleeding along the *entire length* of the cut, sealing it completely; yet the clot must be *confined* to the cut or the entire blood system would solidify, causing death. This complexity has marvelled many who search to understand how such a design evolved.

> The eyeball is a series of discrete systems glued together. The lens gathers and focuses light, the retina senses that light. Along with muscles that focus the lens and turn the eye, tear ducts, eyelids and a range of other components, each of these are separate complex systems that work complimentarily. Yet take away just one of those components and the eye will not work. Like the blood clot, the eye raises questions for evolutionary theory as it illustrates *irreducible complexity* – the whole machine ceasing to function when one part is missing.[5]

This book is not meant to be a science text. (Hey, I can't even remember why water bubbles when it's hot.) But in the questions of the scientific experts a whisper is heard. The size of our moon and the design of the earth's atmosphere[6], the nature of carbon[7], and concepts like the "anthropic principle" and "irreducible complexity" have led more and more of the scientific establishment to hear that whisper of divine involvement too:

One of the world's leading astronomers has declared the big bang a "miracle".[8]

A Nobel-prize winning physicist says that the discoveries of physics "seem to reflect intelligence at work in natural law".[9]

One of the world's leading atheists has stunned the philosophical world by changing his mind on the existence of God after wrestling with the scientific evidence for an intelligent mind behind the universe.[10]

No wonder nature is the "cathedral of choice" for many seeking spiritual fulfilment. Around, within, above and before us lie signs of divine involvement in our existence.

All Icelandic people are nature-lovers.
If they have problems, they can't
handle work or relationships, they
will go for a walk on a mountain, and
they'll come back and it'll be fine. It's
the same occasions when, if you were a
Catholic, you'd go to church.

SINGER, BJORK[11]

[a spiritually-wired humanity]

Divine footprints alongside us, divine whispers around us and divine fingerprints within us. To peek inside the human psyche is to enter another world of design, beauty and complexity. For some social scientists, humanity itself holds clues that a creator is involved in our lives, having shaped some of the hopes and yearnings within.

Signals of Transcendence

Sociologist Peter L Berger once wrote a fascinating little book called *A Rumour of Angels: Modern Society and the Rediscovery of the Supernatural*.[12] In it he describes human behaviours that he believes are "signals of transcendence" – natural experiences that point to a super-natural world beyond. In ordinary, everyday human gestures like laughter, hope and play, Berger hears a whisper of an afterlife longed for in the human soul.

Firstly, Berger talks about the way we *order* ourselves. Our communities and societies are structured to provide order, and when it is lost we experience the panic of chaos. When a child awakes and cries in the night its parent assures the child that everything is all right—that the world is in order so there is nothing to fear. Child psychologists see such assurance as essential for healthy development. But where does this longing for order come from? "Throughout most of human history," Berger suggests, "men have believed that the created order of society, in one way or another, corresponds to an underlying order of the universe, a divine order that supports and justifies all human attempts at ordering." As we order our lives we echo a pattern beyond us – a divine design. "In this frame of reference the natural world in which we are born, love and die is not the only world, but only the foreground of another..."

Next is Berger's argument from *play*. Ever been "lost" in a game of sport, a hobby, or creative endeavour and felt like time has stood still? Joyful play sets up an alternative universe from the "serious" world of work and responsibility. In this universe time takes on an eternal quality – we don't think of 11am but of the third round, the fourth act, the second kiss. Time seems to fly by without our awareness and pain and death seem far away from us. The world of play, for a moment, ushers us into a world characterised by delight, liberation and peace. As we play we experience for a moment what an eternal state of joy might be like. As we play it's as if God opens our eyes to catch a glimpse of heaven.

Third is the human orientation towards *hope*. This is not the trivial "I hope we have good weather for the picnic" use of the word, but the anticipation of a world beyond the grave. Berger notes that human beings have shouted a universal "No!" to death. As he says, it is "in the face of the death of others, and especially of others that we love, that our rejection of death asserts itself most loudly. It is here, above all, that everything we are calls out for a hope that will refute the empirical fact". This death-refusing cry lies at the heart of our being. Why? Our universal "No!" to death hints at a world where death does not have the final say; a world we seem built for.

Closely related to this is the argument for *damnation*. A photograph taken at a mass execution during World War II shows a mother clutching her child. She is supporting the child's body with one arm while firmly pressing its face into her shoulder. A few feet away stands a German soldier with his rifle raised, taking aim. In the case of monstrous evil like this – the gassing of millions of Jews by Nazis, the slaughter of nearly a million Tutsis and moderate Hutus in Rwanda, nearly two million killed by the Cambodian Khmer Rouge – human punishment doesn't seem enough for perpetrators of this kind. Such atrocities trigger an inbuilt cry of the heart for a punishment of supernatural proportions. Perhaps we could say our "No!" to death has a corresponding "Yes!" to ultimate justice beyond this life. The hope is that such tyrants and murderers will get their just deserts when they face their Maker, otherwise the world doesn't make sense.

Finally, Berger talks about *humour* as a signal of transcendence. Most of our humour highlights a discrepancy between the way life is and the way it ought to be. Think about it. What do we laugh at most? Our failures! (Like the granddaughter of a bus driver who said "I want to die peacefully in my sleep like my grandfather... not screaming in terror like his passengers".) It is the imperfect situations in life that make us laugh. The satire of the political cartoonist and the bumbling adventures of a stand-up comic both describe a world of imperfection. In so doing, we affirm the possibility (even the reality) of a perfect world. "The comic reflects the imprisonment of the human spirit in the world," says Berger. "By laughing at the imprisonment of the human spirit, humour implies that this imprisonment is not final but will be overcome."

Our desire for order, our enjoyment of play, our "No!" to death, our "Yes!" to retribution for tyrants and our laughter at imperfection each provide a glimpse of another realm, a whisper of an afterlife, a sign that we long for a heavenly place. These experiences seem hardwired into our humanity as if we were built for the world they point to.

Hardwired for Meaning

Then there are the numerous reports suggesting that spirituality and a "religious" lifestyle holds physical, mental and emotional benefits for us.

For instance, one study suggests that people who attend religious services at least once a week are 28 per cent less likely to die in a given time period than those who don't.[13] Students who do not participate in any religious activities are more than twice as likely to report poor mental health or depression than students who attend religious activities frequently.[14] In general, a higher degree of spirituality correlates with higher self-esteem, more positive attitudes towards the future, lower levels of depression and anxiety, lower blood pressure and a greater sense of wellbeing.

Some scientific studies warn of the long-term effects of secularism on young people. "Denying or ignoring the spiritual need of adolescents," one report said, "may end up creating a void in their lives that either devolves into depression or is filled by other forms of questing and challenge, such as drinking, unbridled consumerism, petty crime, sexual precocity, or flirtations with violence." It is surprising to hear a non-religious research group suggest that "the need in young people to connect to ultimate meaning and to the transcendent is not merely the result of social conditioning, but is instead an intrinsic aspect of the human experience."[15]

I envy people of faith. I'm incapable of believing in anything supernatural. So far, at least. Not that I wouldn't like to. I mean, I want to believe. I do pray. I pray something…up there. I have a God sense. It's not religious so much as superstitious. It's part of being human, I guess…

ACTOR, JACK NICHOLSON[16]

[beauty, pleasure & transendence]

On a holiday to the United Kingdom a few years back, my
wife, a friend and I picked up a hire car and set out for the
Scottish Highlands. Our UK trip had been good up to that
point, but our trek around the Highlands left us awestruck.
For a whole week we feasted on the sensual delights of
Scottish beauty – monstrous mountains with snow-capped
peaks and heather-covered slopes, secluded villages
with pipe-smoking locals, running streams and summer
thunderstorms, ancient cemeteries and historic castles. When
the sun shone every photo turned into a postcard, and when
the rain fell (which it did frequently – the locals said we'd
picked a bad summer) we enjoyed the crisp atmosphere
outside and the warm fires inside our hostel.

On day four of our trip we pulled up in a fishing town called
Ullapool. Finding the local Youth Hostel Association's digs we
lugged our gear inside and set out to see some of this harbour-
side village. Ullapool's main street runs alongside the lake it
lives off and our hostel overlooked its shipping and trawling
activity. After dinner the three of us headed to the common
room for some relaxed trip planning and board games.

Scotland's summer days can last until midnight as daylight
slowly ebbs away. Around 9pm I idly lifted my eyes from the
Scrabble board to gaze out the window. What I saw caught
my breath. "I have never seen that before!" I blurted out in a
rare moment of social forgetfulness. Other guests followed my
gaze out the window and soon there was a rush for the stairs
as people ran for their cameras. Within moments the whole
village was standing on the stone wall alongside the lake with
fingers pointing, cameras snapping, and eyes savouring the
spectacle.

Right there in front of us was the end of a rainbow.

For over an hour the rainbow's colourful beams shone majestically. Its arc stretched from the mountains on our left, rose high into the silver-blue sky, and ended what seemed like a hundred metres or so in front of us on the lake's surface. Before long the entire valley was drenched in an orange-pink glow as the setting sun filtered through the atmosphere. Our camera settings would never record the sight in its fullness. I have never seen anything else like it.

As the boats bobbed on the near-still water and as light reflected all around, a different mood flooded that little town too. The excitement gave way to a certain reverence. With all eyes drawn to a common majestic focal point, the township – for a moment – felt like a united brother and sisterhood. Relational barriers dropped as strangers turned to each other to discuss the awesome sight before them. Some sat in silence. In that hour I think it would've been difficult to continue some previous argument.

At one point I found myself standing next to a Jewish couple I'd met earlier. I wondered if they were thinking what I was. "'Never again will I destroy the world by flood,'" I quoted, recalling the book of Genesis with my eyes fixed on the rainbow.[17] The couple smiled knowingly. Surely we were conscious of something Greater in that moment than simply refracted light waves through an atmosphere of mist.

Beauty as Sign

Our naturalistic assumptions about the world don't explain the beauty of that Ullapool moment very well. There is no real reason to expect beauty to "evolve" – it does not enhance our ability to survive and doesn't really abide by the rules of natural selection. The human ability to *appreciate* beauty raises similar arguments – aesthetic enjoyment is not essential for our existence. Perhaps aesthetic value and its appreciation, again, are more like a gift than the result of cosmic struggles for survival.[18]

The intuitive soul ventures beyond beauty's initial appearance though. A glacier, a rainbow, a classic Renoir – truly aesthetic pieces have a quality that points beyond them. They are signs. A sign can be stared at or it can be followed. I can look at a road sign, see that it is made of thick aluminium sheeting with black polythene letters adhered to a yellow background, fastened by brackets and bolts to two poles supporting it from the ground. Or, I can read the sign's message and follow its directions.

Beauty points to a source. "When we are awed by the intolerable majesty of the Himalaya," said Evelyn Underhill over seven decades ago, "we are merely receiving through symbols adapted to our size, intimations of the Absolute beauty..." In looking at objects of genuine aesthetic value Underhill believed we pass "through and beyond this object, to the experience of an Absolute revealed in things".[19]

The atheist Anthony O'Hear admits as much when he says, "Through art, particularly the great masterpieces of the past, we do have intimations of beauty, of order, of divinity even, way beyond the biological... In responding to our experience of the world in moral and aesthetic ways, we are implying there is something to be responded to... seeing the world as animated by some higher quasi-personal purpose, operating through and behind the material process revealed and studied by natural science."[20]

For those with eyes to see, beauty can reflect God like the moon reflects the sun.

Whispers in Pleasure

Something similar can be said for the experience of pleasure. As author Philip Yancey aptly questions, "Why is sex fun? Reproduction surely does not require pleasure: some animals simply split in half to reproduce, and even humans use methods of artificial insemination that involve no pleasure. Why is eating enjoyable? Plants and the lower animals manage to obtain their quota of nutrients without the luxury of taste buds. Why are there colours? Some people get along fine without the ability to detect colour. Why complicate vision for all the rest of us?"[21]

Renowned for books like *Where is God When it Hurts?* and *Disappointment With God*, Yancey came to these questions after reading the works of the twentieth century writer GK Chesterton. "I had spent a lot of time thinking about the problem of pain. He posed a different kind of problem – what about the problem of pleasure? Why is the world so full of goodness and beauty? I remember a statement from GK Chesterton that just stabbed me in the heart. He said, 'The worst moment for an atheist is when he feels profoundly grateful yet has no one to thank.' I found myself in that state. I felt gratitude, I had encountered some of the beauty and goodness of this world, and I wanted to know the Author who gave it to me, the Creator of it all. And that eventually led me back to God."[22]

God is not necessarily "closer" to us when we reflect on art, enjoy a sumptuous feast or have an Ullapool-type encounter. As Saint Paul put it, God is not far from any of us at any time.[23] But in such moments of pleasure and aesthetic rapture our senses are peculiarly receptive to signals of divine existence. Such experiences awaken us to a greater Someone who is in the world – a Someone we may not have given much attention to before. A Someone who provides good food to eat and joy in our hearts.[24]

It really wasn't through the words of the Church, a Gideon Bible, a Gospel tract or Billy Graham that I came back to faith. It was through "other" words of God: beauty, classical music, nature, romantic love. Those kinds of things awakened me to a world of goodness and beauty, and eventually led me back to the source of that.

AUTHOR, PHILIP YANCEY

[the voice of God]

Creation, humanity, beauty – each whispers to us, hinting
at a God that is active in our lives. Then there are historical
accounts of God speaking to people directly. Such messages
may be more "felt" than heard. Sometimes they have come
through a dream or vision. Occasionally a distinct voice
has been experienced. It seems that the divine chooses, on
occasion, to make himself clearly understood through words,
phrases and syntax. It is here that our "whispers" get a little
louder.

A variety of contemporary and historical identities attest to
this experience:

> A 36 year-old woman devotes fifteen years of her life
> teaching in an Indian school. During a train trip she
> hears a divine call to serve in the nation's slums. She
> obeys, and becomes Mother Teresa of Calcutta.

> On February 7, 1837 a young girl named Florence
> hears a voice calling her to devote her whole life to
> God. As she responds she is filled with great faith
> and confidence, although she has no idea what she
> is supposed to do. But her obedience to that whisper
> pays off. Florence Nightingale later becomes a heroine
> of hospital system reform, touching the lives of
> millions.

> Late one night David Wilkerson opens a copy of *Life*
> magazine and stares at an artist's impression of a boy,
> one of seven on trial for murder. Unexpectedly he
> begins to cry. He hears a persistent command – 'Go to
> New York city and help those boys'. Against all logic
> he obeys. Today, Wilkerson's Teen Challenge centres
> have among the highest success rates of drug and
> alcohol recovery programs in the world.

Many of the world's great humanitarian endeavours have been set in motion because of such whispers to a human soul. But the experience is not limited to the personal and subjective. Researchers have found a recurring voice in the folk religions of tribal groups around the world.

The "Sky-God" Speaks

Consider what anthropologists call the "Sky-God" phenomenon. In his popular book *Eternity In Their Hearts*, Don Richardson presents case after case of a benevolent, all-powerful deity revealing himself to a variety of people groups. While the Sky God may be given a different name by each group – Viracocha (Omnipotent Creator) by the Incas of Peru, Thakur Jiu (Genuine God) by the Santals of India, Magano (Omnipotent Creator of all that is) by the Gedeo people of Ethiopia, Koro (Creator) by the Central African Republic's Mbaka people, Shang Ti (Lord of Heaven) by the Chinese, Hananim (Great One) by the Koreans, Y'wa (True God) by the Burmese Karen peoples – this Being's self-revelation proves mysteriously similar in each case.

For these tribal peoples the Sky-God is understood to be the one uncreated and supreme deity, the giver and sustainer of all life and the one previous tribal generations once knew yet lost touch with through neglect or disobedience. Later religions may have introduced other deities for worship but the ancient folk religion for each group had this one distinct Person in its history. In most of these tribes there was a desire to be reconciled with this Being; their devotion to "lesser" gods done more out of fear than love.

Unrelated and largely distanced from each other geographically, these tribes had remarkably similar legends and prophecies relating to this Person. The Santals and Karens had Creation and Flood stories similar to the Genesis record of Jews and Christians. India's Mizo and Naga people, the Chinese Lisu, the Kui on the Thai-Burma border, and the Wa, Kachin and Lahu tribes all anticipated promised messengers who would bring "the book" of teaching about the supreme God to them. Many anticipated the true God reconciling their previous misdeeds by some special event. The Mbaka tribesman believed that Koro, the Creator, had sent his son into the world to accomplish "something wonderful" for all humankind. Richardson recounts the words of Mbaka tribesman: "Since the time of 'the forgetting' successive generations of our people have longed to discover the truth about Koro's Son. But all we could learn was that messengers would eventually come to restore that forgotten knowledge to us."[25]

Anticipated Messengers, Mysterious Miracles

In fact, the prediction of "coming messengers" is a repeated phenomenon in these situations too. Though regarded as distant and more or less unreachable, this Sky-God tends to draw near and speak whenever seekers of truth are, unknowingly, about to meet messengers bearing the truth they seek.

Missionary Ben Staggs describes such an experience when visiting the Boshu people, an extremely isolated group in Ethiopia's Me'en territory. On arrival, Ben and his team were welcomed by a local named Golon Kabule. "We sat down and spoke a bit," says Ben, "explaining that we had come to tell them of 'God's talk'. I described who God is, what He is like, and where He lives." But Golon hardly needed informing. He suddenly spoke up. "We must follow Christosi [the Me'en word for Christ]," he said. Astonished, as Christ's name had not even been mentioned, Ben asked where Golon had heard that name. Golon explained that Christ had appeared to him in a dream, told him that it was he who had given Golon his life, blood and bones, and that Golon was to follow him. Christ then said that in just five days someone would come to tell him about following that path. Ben and his team had landed on the fifth day after the dream.[26]

There are hundreds, even thousands, of reports of people around the world having such experiences. The encounters have a similar theme – Christ appears and issues a straightforward call to follow him.

Sounds dodgy? I admit that when I hear such stories scepticism weighs in. I wonder about the motives of the story tellers and the trustworthiness of the media that carry their tales. I can have vivid dreams too – particularly following a large Pepperoni Supreme or a good red curry. But for most there is little to be gained by fabricating such a story. In fact, for those in religiously restricted countries, declaring such an experience could mean torture or death, harsh punishment for abandoning the culturally-accepted deities.

But some of these dreams are coming accompanied by more tangible evidence of divine encounter – physical healings.

"My father, for instance," says Pakistani-born Dr. Michael Nazir-Ali, now a church leader, "was baptized in a church that had been built by a Muslim noble woman who had been healed as a result of a vision of Jesus. She never became a Christian as far as I know, but she built this Christian church as a thank offering. There are many, many such people." According to Nazir-Ali, some do something about their dream or vision and others don't. "In one case, a man who had a vision of Jesus in the middle of an Islamic city where there was no church travelled hundreds of miles to find a church to ask what he should do. The result is, in that city where he lives, there is a church of about forty people who have all had similar experiences."[27]

What about Westerners?

Such encounters seem to be occurring rapidly in Middle Eastern and Asian countries. (Perhaps they're searching for God more earnestly?) But in no way is the divine voice stifled for those in the West.

I remember hearing Shona's story one Sunday morning in 1999. "All my material, intellectual, family and selfish needs were being met," she said to us listening in the church auditorium, "but there was definitely something more I needed, and my constant searching for this missing element was driving me nuts." Enrolling her daughter in a Christian school, Shona decided to take a course on the Christian faith[28] to prepare for any tricky questions asked by her daughter in the future. About four weeks into the course, Shona had a dream that metaphorically and literally shook her awake. Here's Shona's description:

> In my dream I was at a fabulous party having a wonderful time, when I heard a quiet knock at the door. I opened the door and there was this person. He wasn't tremendously tall or anything but he really stood out because he was so radiant with such a clear white light. There were a couple of figures behind him, but they just faded into insignificance compared to him. "Wow," I said, "I want a piece of what you have. I want to be like you." "You can," he said, and reached over and touched me above the heart. I looked down and I could see into my heart and there was a spark of his light there, and I knew it could grow. I woke bolt upright at about 2:30 in the morning and I realised then that was Jesus Christ himself talking to me. That was when I truly asked him to take control of me and to be with me always. I've since found the start of my dream echoes some words in the biblical book of Revelation chapter 3, verse 20: *Behold, I stand at the door and knock. If anyone hears my voice and opens the door, I will come in to him and dine with him, and he with me.*[29]

[holy messengers]

The divine being seems to be speaking to us through nature,
laughter, play; through our future hopes, through beauty
and pleasure and occasionally through direct address. Then
there are divinely-inspired people who cross the threshold
of our lives, touch us deeply, and leave us with a sense that
through their actions we've actually encountered Someone
else too.

Time to finish the story of Johnny Lee Clary, of the Ku
Klux Klan...

To you, O my heart, he has said,
"Seek my face!"
Your face, Lord, I will seek.

ANCIENT HEBREW SONG[30]

A Grandmother and a Black Preacher

"The Klan was there for me when no one else was," Johnny reminded himself when he questioned KKK behaviour. But there were two people who did stick by him. One was an enemy; the other, his grandmother.

"She reminded me of Granny on *The Beverly Hillbillies*," Johnny remembers of his grandmother. Seeing her grandson in the papers promoting the Klan would break her heart. "She'd say to me, 'Boy, you shouldn't hate other people like that. Johnny, get out of that mess'. I'd say, 'Oh, you just don't understand. Besides, I'm going to be Governor of Oklahoma some day'. And she'd reply, 'Boy, you wouldn't make a pimple on a Governor's behind. But if you're going to insist on belonging to the Klan I'm going to go pray for you!'"

Pray she did – for years.

Then came Johnny's invitation to join a debate on a national radio talk show. Through that debate Johnny would come face to face with a black civil rights leader, the Reverend Wade Watts. It would be an experience that would change his life.

"I thought Reverend Watts would show up wearing a giant afro and an African dashiki, wearing a button that said 'I Hate Honkys' and carrying a boom box playing the theme from *Shaft*. Instead, here was a nicely dressed man in a suit and a tie and carrying a Bible in his hand. He walked up to me, put out his hand and said, 'Hello Mr. Clary. I just want you to know that I love you and Jesus loves you'."

The on-air debate went back and forth, Johnny stating reasons why the races should have nothing to do with each other, and Reverend Watts politely refuting each claim from Scripture. Afterwards, as Johnny made his way through the station lobby to leave, the reverend appeared with a baby in his arms. "Mr. Clary, this is my daughter Tia," he said. "And I have one last question for you." He held out the little girl. "You say you hate all black people, Mr. Clary. Just tell me – how can you hate this child?"

Stunned, Johnny almost ran out of the station. "Nothing you do can make me hate you," the reverend called out after him. "I'm going to love you and pray for you, Mr. Clary, whether you like it or not!"

Along with climbing the Klan's ranks, Johnny's burning goal from that moment on was to make Reverend Watts pay for that experience in the radio station. Klansmen made threatening phone calls to Watts' family. His windows were broken, effigies were torched on his lawn, they burnt down one of his Baptist churches and set fire to another. The thirteen Watts children (a number of whom were adopted) had to be escorted to school by authorities.

But nothing stopped the reverend in his mission of justice or his loving response to enemies. And Johnny never forgot the way the reverend had treated him that day, trading compliment for insult, blessing for curse.

Johnny's destructive lifestyle began to take its toll. Riddled with anger over a false arrest for a weapons violation, disgusted by internal fighting between white supremacist organisations, and discovering that his girlfriend was an informant for the FBI, led Johnny to resign from the Klan. But the pain would continue. Over the next few years he found himself dealing with the loss of a daughter and the end of a marriage.

These losses, combined with obsessive guilt over the life of hatred he'd lived, led Johnny to alcohol for comfort. Finally, it seemed life was not worth the effort. Johnny found himself in his shabby apartment raising a loaded gun to his head, preparing to follow in his father's footsteps.

Moments away from pulling the trigger sunlight broke through some partially closed blinds, illuminating an old Bible on Johnny's bookshelf. "A Bible like the one Reverend Watts carried that day at the radio station," he remembers. "A Bible like the one I had seen my grandmother read so many times." Maybe there was another way. Johnny put down the gun and picked up the Bible. It fell open to Luke chapter 15, the story of the prodigal son. He read the story three times, then fell on his knees and wept.

Johnny quietly joined a church with a multi-racial congregation (no small step considering his background) and kept a low profile. Two years passed, and then in 1991 he made a phone call.

"Reverend Watts?" Johnny asked when the phone picked up. He hadn't seen the civil rights leader in thirteen years but the preacher knew Johnny's voice right away. "Hello, Johnny Lee," he said warmly. "Reverend Watts," Johnny said, "I want you to know that I got out of the Klan two years ago." "That's good," replied the reverend. "And I've been attending a multiracial church." "That's good!" cried Reverend Watts.

When Johnny added that he now felt a calling (a whisper!) to speak about God and the Bible, Reverend Watts made an outrageous offer. "Have you spoken anywhere yet, son?" he asked. "How about you give me the honour of preaching your very first time in my all-black church." So the ex-Imperial Wizard of the Ku Klux Klan took the podium of the same church he had once set fire to.

Looking out over the congregation of mostly black faces, Johnny told his story simply. He had hated black people, but God had changed the hate in his heart to love. After recounting further details of his conversion, Johnny finished his message.

There was silence. The congregation considered his story, and some were obviously cynical.

Then a teenage girl got to her feet and ran down the church aisle, her arms open. Johnny moved towards her thinking she was coming forward to be prayed for or counselled. Then he saw that Reverend Watts was weeping. "Don't you know who that is, Johnny Lee?" the reverend asked quietly.

"That's Tia. That's my baby."

Johnny Lee Clary heard a whisper that led to life. He heard that whisper through a grandmother who refused to give up on him while others said he was too lost to save. He heard that whisper through the life and actions of a black preacher who radiated sacrificial love, who refused to retaliate, who loved his enemy. Johnny caught a whisper of transforming love uttered through human intermediaries. Responding to that voice, he experienced a transformation of heart.[31]

Have you heard a whisper yet?

Perhaps God has spoken to you even this week without you realizing it.

Nature and humanity, beauty and pleasure, heavenly voices and the God-like actions of others – as I ponder each it's as if they gradually change form. I see the rainforest, but the longer I look it begins to fade. I consider a piece of art, and it slowly disappears. I reflect on the Wade Watts of the world and they gradually diminish. Each dissolves to a transparency through which I see their author, their model, their first cause – an all-powerful Person who is separate from and yet the source of each one's profound influence. Each becomes a window to another world. Each calls for our attention like a quiet voice along a lonely passageway.

And what is this voice saying?

You're special to me.

I made this world especially for you. (Do you think I need a universe?)

Your body and soul, no matter your weight or appearance, are fashioned in my image.

Beauty and pleasure are your gifts.

If you come close, I'll whisper into your soul my purpose for your life. But I will not shout to make myself heard. The ball's in your court. Do you really want to know me?

I haven't anything conclusive
to say to you about the subject
[of spirituality]... My state
is seeking, and I haven't yet
come to an arrival point. And
it's a little late, because time is
running out and if I don't come
to an arrival point soon, I'm
leaving the planet and I haven't
understood anything.

SINGER-SONGWRITER, ANNIE LENNOX

>>>**CHAPTER FOUR**
ENCOUNTER:
JOURNEY
INTERRUPTED

So we find ourselves on this journey, with our aches and limps and yearnings. And if we take

a moment to listen we find that God is whispering to us, through words and experiences and people. And we find ourselves with a choice to make: We can stop, listen and respond to God, or we can walk on, hitch our horse and cart, and continue down the dusty highway of our lives.

We can accept the invitation to divine relationship or reject it.

The ball's in your court, God tells us.

Yet something in us commonly holds back from responding to the divine. What is it? When it seems our very lives are designed for such a relationship and when our yearnings have failed to be met by other means, why would we turn our backs and stride on?

Following my abandonment of DJ dreams, I found that decision point before me – to stop and respond, or walk and ignore. With my life feeling bankrupt I was warming to the idea of divine assistance. But I was wary. The greater part of me wanted to try another path of my own making; to try any alternative to what could be perceived as "getting religious".

[fearing God for all the wrong reasons]

As many a pilgrim can attest, there are forces at work to distract us from this moment of divine encounter. And the greatest of these forces is fear.

Part of our reticence to respond to God may be a fear of what he might require of us if we do. Will we have to wear an orange robe, twist into the lotus position and sell flowers at train stations? Will we have to cut our hair short, ride a bicycle and wear a name badge with "Elder Smith" on it?

We can fear what others will think of us. Will family reject us when we share our experiences? Will friends distance themselves, fearing we've become recruiters for a religious sales force?

And some of us fear God himself. Burnt by past experiences of religion, a lonely, dusty road holds much greater attraction than returning to a god of anger, whose representatives rule by force, fear and guilt.

I felt many of these fears at my point of decision. I wondered how my life would have to change. I wondered what others would think of me. And, like many, I still had a sour taste in my mouth from the religious experience of my youth.

[feeling trapped]

I remember once, as a six or seven year old, lying in my bed feeling hopeless. At the time my parents were involved in one of the world's more zealous religious sects, and I was being raised according to its tenets.

The sect was very strict. Tracing the origins of Christmas trees and Easter eggs back to pagan practices, devotees were forbidden to celebrate such festivals. Birthday parties were out too, the religion's leaders citing some obscure verse from the Old Testament (which I still haven't found) to teach that one day should not be lifted in significance above another. Growing up I'd feel a certain discomfort as these celebrations approached. On Christmas Day I'd watch as other kids played with their new presents. I'd wish friends a "happy holiday" instead of "Happy Easter". I didn't have birthday parties and rarely attended others'. While my parents did all they could to make sure I didn't miss out – giving me surprise gifts and holding parties for me at other times – it wasn't hard to feel a little alienated growing up.

When it came time for Religious Instruction class at school, I'd saunter off to E Block to receive a lesson with the three or four other children associated with my faith. Of the seven years I attended these classes I only remember one such lesson – on sex. The teacher, who always looked a little downcast, explained that if us kids ever had sex outside of marriage God would punish us by making the girl involved fall pregnant. I do wonder if any of my peers broke the rule in consequent years. Pity the child whose parents look on them as the sign of divine wrath.

Books and magazines published by the sect's head office were voraciously studied by the faithful. These publications were essential to understanding God, it was taught, as they were the official teachings of the church's inspired hierarchy.

The Bible was read intensely – a special version with some key verses slightly modified to suit the organisation's doctrine. On weekends the disciples dressed in nice clothes, ties and wide-brimmed hats to knock on doors, sell their magazines and spread the word of God.

The sad fact is that many of these followers live with a heavy weight on their hearts, despite their effort and dedication. Deep down they fear they have never done enough to earn God's approval. Have they visited enough neighbours, sold enough magazines, conducted enough studies or won enough converts? On the day of Armageddon, when God judges who is fit for life and who is fit for eternal destruction, will they make it through? Some are never sure, which makes them work even harder.

As I lay in my bed that night as a primary schooler, I realised I was trapped. To have any chance of gaining God's favour I'd have to knock on strangers' doors every weekend, trying to convert people. I didn't want to do that – I felt too shy. But if I didn't, it seemed God would be angry with me. Then again, I could visit every home in my town and there was still no promise that God would accept me.

Either way, it seemed I was heading for hell.

And life began to look like a sick joke.

I rolled over and tried to think of other things – roller skating, Lego, my Hot Wheels collection. Facing an angry and unfair God was just too scary a thought for this second-grader.

As human knowledge has grown,
it has also become plain that
every religious story ever told
about how we got here is quite
simply wrong... I think it is true
that on the subject of religion,
clearly I've had rather a course of
aversion therapy to it. No doubt
that shows.

AUTHOR, SALMAN RUSHDIE[1]

I once heard of a private school pupil who was punished for not remembering one of her Bible verses. "God is love! God is love! God is love!" the nun reminded her – as she hit the student across the knuckles with a ruler. Imagine the Pavlovian effect that phrase has on the student today: God is love – he makes my hands bleed.

Unfortunately, every religion and philosophy has its hucksters, impostors, and other simply misguided souls lurking around its edges. These are people whose actions mismatch their doctrines. Charismatic personalities who wield the name of God as a weapon of control. Entrepreneurs who see dollar signs attached to spiritual need. Whether it's a little boy cowering from an unpleasable God, a pupil suffering at the hands of ecclesiastical authority, or a hurting woman fleeced of her money by a New Age guru, many have been introduced through such people to a god they'd now rather avoid. Still flinching from their wounds they quickly retreat when the divine name is mentioned.

But others have denied the hucksters a final win. Their wallets empty and their hearts a little scarred, they forge on nevertheless in their search to encounter the divine.

To find the true God.

Not the god of the impostors.

In my opinion, there are two essential problems with believing God is somebody He isn't. The first problem is that it wrecks your life, and the second is that it makes God look like an idiot.

AUTHOR, DONALD MILLER[2]

[spotting the authentic God]

As any psychologist can tell you, our understanding of God is vitally important. Many are held captive by an imaginary deity shaped by the fear and pain of their past – like the "angry father"god or the "you-must-be-perfect" god. Others bow to a spirit fashioned from personal wishes and desires – perhaps the "success and riches" god or the "do-as-you-please" god. These humanly-inspired gods will always break our hearts, either failing to meet our expectations or forever holding us in torment. For our soul's sake, we need to get God right.

To find life and freedom we'll need to spot the authentic God, a quest that may seem difficult in the face of the multitude of religions, spiritualities and belief systems surrounding us. But if God's unseen footprints are truly woven through our lives, he is not that far away from us. And if the divine has already been whispering to us, getting our attention, then God seems to be searching for us as much we are for him.

Sooner or later, then, we should bump into him.

Whispers and the Nature of God

But let's start with what we already know about the divine. If the authentic God has been whispering to us, his character will already be evident to some extent. The mouth speaks from the overflow of the heart.[3] A football fan will talk more about sport than an artist will; the infatuated will talk plenty about their beloved. If the content and tone of our speech reflects something of our heart, it follows that the whispers of the divine will reflect something of his personality too. What might God's whispers reveal about him?

If God has whispered through our world and cosmos, then we see a *God of power, intelligence and creativity*. Only a deity of such qualities could envision both the beauty of a Saturn and the intricacy of a DNA string. Only an imaginative, design-conscious God could invent the eyeball, the sun, the nervous system and the snowflake.

If the authentic God has whispered through the assortment of animal breeds, plant life, skin colours and human personalities in this world, then we see a *God of variety and diversity*. Only such a Being would shape each life form to a basic pattern, but add an infinite array of subtle difference to each.

If the authentic God has whispered through beauty and pleasure, we see *a God who values aesthetics and expression; a deity who must love fun and joy and excitement*. Only such a God would create the tonal differences of musical notes, the textures and colours of dirt and the enjoyment experienced in laughter. Only such a deity would assign pleasure to hobbies, invigoration to sports and contentment to eating.

If the authentic God has whispered to us in our hopes – if our anticipation of an afterlife has a corresponding heaven, and our longing for evil's end a corresponding judgement – we see *a God who is good and just*. This judge will not turn a blind eye to greed and vice. Secret deals will not remain hidden. Victims will be vindicated and the poor liberated. There will be justice in the end.

And if the earth really has been crafted for human living and the human soul truly crafted for spiritual living, we are dealing *with a God who is personal*. This God is more than energy or a life force. If this Being cares enough to inspire a grandmother and a black preacher to love a Ku Klux Klan Imperial Wizard, if he speaks to the leaders of tribes and to searching suburban housewives, if he would extend an invitation to an empty-hearted DJ to find life, we see a God who gives himself for others' benefit.

We see a God who *loves*.

For most of us it takes a lifetime
to realise we're like kids walking
through the precinct holding our
Daddy's hand. We can only see his
knees. When I was converted at 16 I
knew everything... Now that I'm 52
I know nothing. Except that I think
there probably is a God and I think
he's probably quite nice.

COMEDIAN, ADRIAN PLASS

[moving on from the vague God]

When we reflect on the words and whispers of the divine we glimpse something of the person uttering them. If we've heard correctly, God seems to be a powerful, personal and loving character. But can we know more?

A number of years back JB Phillips wrote a perceptive little book called *Your God Is Too Small*. In it he talked of "little gods that infect human minds". Amongst other things, he exposed the anaemia of the "Meek and Mild" god, the fear and guilt behind the "Resident Policeman" god, and the psychological projection of the "Parental Hangover" god. Phillips' classic book gives an insight into those humanly constructed gods that will ultimately break our hearts.

Moving on from these distortions, Phillips then wonders how the authentic God can be known. In a similar journey to the one we've taken, he discovers "clues" to God's nature in experiences like beauty and goodness and truth. But such concepts remain abstract and unfocused. For humans to truly understand these values they need to be embodied. "We can visualise a beautiful thing, but not beauty," Phillips surmised, "a good man, but not goodness; a true fact, but not truth... Absolute values may exist as mental concepts for the trained philosopher; but the ordinary man must see his values focused in people or things that he knows before he can grasp them."[4]

For humans to truly understand God, Phillips then imagines, God would need to embody himself somehow. As a rose gives a face to beauty, only an embodied God could be truly comprehensible to us.

God Embodied in Story

Occasionally, writers through the ages have caught something of the divine Being and embodied their revelations into story. CS Lewis was one of those writers, and his children's classic *The Lion, The Witch and The Wardrobe* is one of those stories. It's a tale that takes us a step closer in understanding who God might be.

Lewis' tale begins with four children, Peter, Susan, Edmund and Lucy, who are sent away from London because of the war. They are sent to the countryside and stay in the mansion of an eccentric professor. Exploring the many halls and passageways of the home the children discover a room containing a wardrobe, and once Lucy ventures inside she discovers the wardrobe to be a doorway to a magical land named Narnia.

Narnia is an enchanted place with a wide range of unusual inhabitants and talking animals. But Narnia has a dark side. An evil Witch holds control and has hexed the land into a perpetual winter. Narnia's inhabitants await the return of their king, an awesome and majestic Lion named Aslan. When Aslan roars, every discussion is silenced. It was he who had sung Narnia into existence and brought its animals and wildlife out of the ground.[5] It was he who would someday restore Narnia and deal with the White Witch. And so when the rumour spreads that Aslan has been seen in Narnia, anticipation grows throughout the land.

Edmund is walking in Narnia's forest one day when he meets the Witch. Plying him with free Turkish Delight and promises of making him king of the land, the Witch entices Edmund to bring the rest of the children back to her. His mind consumed with extra sweets and the superiority royalty would bring him, he agrees. It doesn't take long, however, for Edmund to discover the Witch's true nature.

She abuses him and never delivers on her promises. But by then he is enslaved.

Lucy, Susan and Peter go in search of Edmund, and having been granted an audience with the returned Aslan, are accompanied by the Lion on their search.

While Edmund is found and initially saved from the Witch's hands, there are legal consequences to his actions. Under Narnian law Edmund's life can only be redeemed by another. "You know that every traitor belongs to me as my lawful prey and that for every treachery I have a right to kill," the Witch reminds Aslan as they stand off. "And so that human creature is mine. His life is forfeit to me... unless I have blood as the Law says all Narnia will be overturned and perish in fire and water."

The Lion and the Witch discuss the situation in private and arrive at an agreement. Edmund will be released from his fate, but the Law will be upheld. Another will die in Edmund's place.

From that point, Aslan's mood changes. Unable to sleep one evening, Susan and Lucy get up and catch Aslan walking slowly away from their camp. His tail droops and his head hangs low enough for his nose to touch the grass.

"Are you ill, dear Aslan?" Susan asks.

"No," Aslan replies. "I am sad and lonely. Lay your hands on my mane so that I can feel you are there and let us walk like that."

Walking a little while further, Aslan dismisses the girls and approaches a giant altar known as the Stone Table. A large crowd of creatures surround it; dark beings like ogres and wolves and the spirits of evil trees. And standing next to the Table is the Witch herself.

"The fool!" the Witch cries as she spots Aslan. "The fool has come. Bind him fast."

The Witch's helpers run to Aslan, push him onto his back and bind all four paws together. The chords are pulled tight, so tight they cut into his flesh. As Aslan is dragged towards the Stone Table there is no fight or mighty roar. He willingly submits to his fate. On the Witch's command an ogre takes a pair of shears and attacks Aslan's majestic mane. The golden fur falls and the Lion is humiliated as the crowds laugh and taunt.

Aslan is finally lifted onto the altar. The Witch takes her whetted knife, raises her hand and kills Narnia's lion-ruler. The king dies for Edmund. The Witch and her rabble fly off into the night, intent on controlling Narnia now that its leader is eliminated. With the area clear, Susan and Lucy come out of their hiding place and sit weeping and stroking Aslan's now cold head.

Hours pass, and when the girls have no tears left they get up for a walk. But as they wander from the execution scene, a sudden loud cracking noise erupts from behind them. The girls run back to find the Stone Table broken in two, split from end to end, with no sign of Aslan's body.

"What does it mean?" cries Susan. "Is it more magic?"

"Yes!" comes a powerful voice from behind them.

The girls turn, and there in the sunrise stands Aslan, shaking his perfectly restored mane.

And Narnia soon shakes under the power of a loud and ferocious roar.

At the name of Aslan each one of the children felt something jump in its inside. Edmund felt a sensation of mysterious horror. Peter felt suddenly brave and adventurous. Susan felt as if some delicious smell or some delightful strain of music had just floated by her. And Lucy got the feeling you have when you wake up in the morning and realize that it is the beginning of the holidays or the beginning of summer.

THE LION, THE WITCH AND THE WARDROBE[6]

[God embodied in humanity]

If you have ever read *The Lion, The Witch and The Wardrobe*
you will know the outcome of Aslan's miraculous return.
Edmund's debt is paid, the Witch's fate is sealed and Narnia's
perpetual winter is lifted. But what you may not know is that
it came from CS Lewis experiencing something of a divine
encounter himself.

CS Lewis was a literary scholar at the prestigious Oxford
University. When JRR Tolkien came to teach at Oxford
the two men struck a deep friendship, regularly critiquing
and encouraging each other's writing. In fact, it is unlikely
Tolkien's famous *Lord of the Rings* would have made it to print
without Lewis' encouragement.

Through a series of events, Lewis began to question his
long-held atheism. In his early biography *Surprised By Joy*, he
describes being hounded by God "night after night, feeling,
whenever my mind lifted even for a second from my work,
the steady, unrelenting approach of Him whom I so earnestly
desired not to meet." Lewis finally gave in to his pursuer and
conceded that there was a God; "perhaps, that night, the most
dejected and reluctant convert in all England."[7]

But Lewis' understanding of God was vague at this point.
He described God as "the Absolute", the one true concept
behind the world, but wasn't sure if that concept was
personal. He continued to talk to Tolkien about the divine;
their conversation culminating in a now historic evening
in September of 1931. Tolkien and Hugo Dyson walked
with Lewis around Oxford, sharing their views on the New
Testament gospels. These biblical stories describing the life
of Jesus Christ, Tolkien argued, had all the best qualities of
ancient mythical literature but with the unique feature that
the events actually happened. This ignited Lewis' imagination
while challenging his beliefs about the Bible. A couple of days
later Lewis came to the conclusion that Jesus was who these
gospels described him to be – the Son of God.

Lewis didn't intentionally set out to incorporate his spiritual discoveries into *The Lion, The Witch and The Wardrobe* or the rest of the Narnia Chronicles. But as he was writing the story, he says, suddenly "Aslan came bounding into it."[8] Now welcomed by Lewis, Aslan became a picture of God, an image that bears many of the qualities we saw earlier about the divine presence behind the universe:

- Aslan is *powerful*, the ultimate ruler whom all creatures finally answer to.

- Aslan is *creative*, singing Narnia into being and raising its variety of inhabitants from the ground.

- Aslan is not a force or concept, but a *personality* who feels and wants relationship. ("Lay your hands on my mane so I can feel you are there…")

- And Aslan depicts *self-giving love*, taking the penalty of Edmund's actions on himself and dying in his place for no personal gain.

Yet *The Lion, The Witch and The Wardrobe* is not a new story. Aslan's power, creativity and love echo another older tale, an ancient account which has inspired women and men through the ages – the story of Easter.

- The story of a man who took the penalty of humankind's rebellious actions on himself, dying a cruel, humiliating death for no personal gain.

- The story of an empty tomb, that same man miraculously resurrected back to life to defeat death itself.

- The story of Jesus, who came bounding into Lewis's life that week in September 1931.

Yes, Lewis based his Aslan character on Christ. Lewis's journey had led to the belief that there was a God and that this God had once embodied himself in humanity. For him, the vague God had become clear, the divine Absolute had been given a face, and Lewis had finally discovered his pursuer.

That there's a force of love and logic
behind the universe is overwhelming
to start with, if you believe it. But
the idea that that same love and
logic would choose to describe itself
as a baby born in s— and straw and
poverty, is genius. And brings me to
my knees, literally.

U2'S BONO[9]

[journey redirected]

As I grappled with my childhood recollections of God and the fears I had about responding to the whispers I was sensing, a funny thing happened. My mother had a divine encounter herself. Like CS Lewis, this encounter altered the course of her life. Like Lewis, the encounter was preceded by some years of questioning long-held beliefs. And just like Lewis, her encounter came as a result of discovering the identity of Jesus.[10]

Through that discovery, my mother (and later my father) was liberated from fear, condemnation and confusion. When you see a life change before your eyes like that you tend to take notice. It can even inspire you to ask a question and read a book or two.

"Without the Bible there would be no Bob Dylan," U2's Bono said a couple of years back. Seeing the effects of its message on those around me, I began to explore the book that inspired the Dylans, Bonos, Michelangelos and Luther-Kings of the world. And like Bono, I found this sacred text to be "like a mirror – you read it and you see your face, sometimes distorted, sometimes clear."[11] Becoming engrossed in the Bible's grand unfolding story I began to see myself and the distortions I lived, but I also began to see God and the distortions about him I'd earlier believed.

There were parts of the Bible which I found difficult to read. Like Edmund hearing Aslan's name for the first time, occasionally I felt a 'mysterious horror' contemplating who these pages described God to be. I found him to be a God of standards whose directives are to be obeyed,[12] a God who had the right to take life as well as give it,[13] and a God of justice whom everyone (me included) would one day answer to.[14] I read that God was truly almighty and not to be treated with reckless indifference. After all, he is the one who decides our ultimate destiny.[15] This was not a cute and cuddly pussycat god that I could stroke and feed and train. As Narnia's Mr. Beaver described Aslan, "He's wild, you know. Not like a *tame* lion."[16]

Yet, in reading this book I discovered a God who is this *and more.* He is awesome and powerful, but also slow to get angry, full of mercy and compassion, and quick to forgive.[17] He is a God who knows us intimately – every thought, action and mannerism – and who draws close when we call for him.[18] This God is concerned for the poor, the orphaned and widowed, and expects us to be concerned for them as well.[19] He counts every tear we shed, feels every moment of grief, and has a plan to make us whole in body, mind and spirit. This God is powerful, yes. But he is kind. In fact, the only word that truly sums him up is *love.*[20]

Motivated by his innate love, this God became a human to live what we live and feel what we feel. While on earth he confronted the religious hucksters and impostors, accepted the rejected and outcast, and embraced the drunk and prostitute as much as the rich and powerful. He confronted racism, denounced hypocrisy and empowered women. He wept with grieving friends, healed the crippled and infirm, and fed the hungry. Then, as foes accused and friends fled, this God submitted to the most torturous treatment ever unleashed on a life – crucifixion on two bits of wood with rusty iron nails.

Yet, he refused to roar.

He restrained his power because this agony was his mission. He arrived to take the punishment for us Edmunds who have chosen our own way instead of his and have so often broken his heart. But when the work was done, when human shame was dealt with and cosmic forces subdued, he bounded back to life, making death the final victim. And for those who want in on the relationship, this God offers a similar promise of full life and an ultimately deathless existence.[21]

New Beginnings

If God really had visited the earth in human form, if he really had shouldered the punishment for every act of greed, pride and harm I'd done, and if forgiveness really was a gift now ready to be received, then this was a God I could give my life to. The night came when, like CS Lewis, I gave in to the divine whisperer who now had a face – the face of Jesus. This new beginning of mine took the form of a simple prayer. I asked forgiveness for thinking I could live life without God. I thanked God for the great sacrifice he'd done for me. And I offered him the management of my life – it was now his to direct as he wanted.

See, God didn't want me to knock on doors, cut my hair or sell flowers at train stations. He doesn't have a series of hoops for us to jump through before we earn his approval. This powerful, creative, personal God wants only one thing:

Us.

Come to me, he says. *I have plans to give your life purpose, hope, and a future that you haven't even dreamt of. I want to write the script of your life into a new and vibrant drama.*

Like feeling the warm breath of Aslan on your face, I have since discovered that nothing compares to the companionship of God.

Nothing compares to journeying alongside the divine whisperer with the human face.

God, you see, rushes to us at the first hint of our openness. He is the hound of heaven baying relentlessly upon our track. And he places within us such an insatiable God hunger that absolutely nothing satisfies us except [him].

AUTHOR, RICHARD FOSTER[22]

>>>CHAPTER FIVE

DOUBT: THE
JOURNEY'S CRISIS

Having encountered the divine
we discover that God's footprints are no longer
circling around us, shuffling in and out of our story as if he
was still getting our attention. The footprints are alongside
us now, and just a step or two ahead. They are leading us
along new passageways, through new terrain, guiding us to
new vistas. Having responded to God's invitation we find
ourselves going in a new direction.

Yet no one who embarks on this journey of divine
companionship can expect to walk unchallenged. Along
these new passageways will be voices – some recognisable
to us, others heard like faceless shouts in a crowded subway
– questioning, testing, sometimes scoffing at our new
direction. Friends and colleagues may recite their accusations
against God as we share our newfound discovery with them.
Academics and family members may express incredulity at
a belief in unseen footprints. And occasionally, one of those
doubting voices will be our own. With a few cuts, bruises,
and questions left unanswered, we may soon find ourselves
sitting in the jury questioning God, unsure about our
discovery, experiencing doubt.

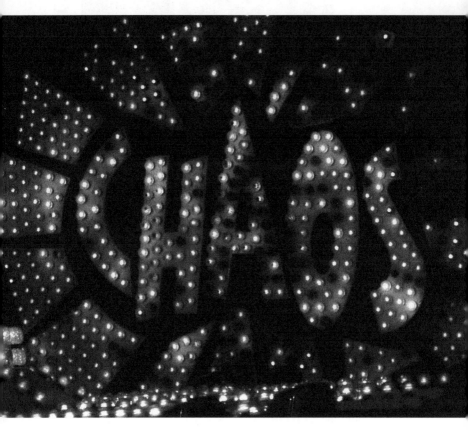

Even if God exists, he's done such a terrible job, it's a wonder people don't get together and file a class-action suit against him.

WOODY ALLEN'S CHARACTER IN *EVERYONE SAYS I LOVE YOU*

[God on trial]

As I've journeyed with others who have encountered the person of Jesus, I have discovered that divine companionship does not magically erase our capacity to feel pain or our ability to get confused. God is not some kind of cosmic serum anaesthetising us from the stings of life. Neither does he turn us into cyborgs whose mental capacities are overridden by his own intellect; unthinking automatons regurgitating the Great Mind's comprehensions on the great philosophical mysteries of existence. Instead, God walks with us through the torrents of life, shaping us through the battles, perfecting us through the trials. Like a father to a child, he spends a lifetime imparting wisdom to us.

Yet many put God on trial. And such a trial usually comes from two main causes.

A Suffering Planet

In Mark Joffe's movie *The Man Who Sued God*, Scottish comedian Billy Connolly plays Steve Myers, a one-time lawyer who's swapped the courtroom for the ocean and become a free-spirited fisherman. But when Myers' fishing boat is destroyed by a lightning strike, his insurance company stalls on the payout. Pointing to the fine print in their contract about damage caused by natural disasters, the insurers deem Myers' loss an 'act of God' and refuse financial responsibility. Infuriated, Myers concocts a plan. He reregisters as a lawyer and heads to court – to sue God.

To prosecute the divine being, Myers summons to court the Anglican, Catholic and Presbyterian churches along with leaders of the Jewish faith. Myers' reasoning goes like this: If God really did destroy his boat, then God's earthly representatives are liable for its replacement. Then again, if God isn't responsible, the insurance companies hide behind a lie and are liable for the boat and every other claim previously rejected under the Act of God clause. The storyline poses a beautiful twist– to win the court battle the churches will have to prove that God does not exist, while the insurance companies will have to prove that he does!

The Man Who Sued God isn't one of the most remarkable films ever created, but its central theme cleverly portrays the essence of doubt in relation to spiritual matters. Disaster and loss naturally raise questions about God. Is he the cause of destructive lightning bolts, and therefore capricious? Or is God a neat human invention, crafted to deflect personal responsibility? (As Steve Myers says early in the film, "I'm not really suing God, you know. I just hate the way people use God as some kind of giant all-purpose lying mechanism.")

Seasons of suffering and experiences of loss may test our faith. Times will come when we wonder where God is, what he's doing and why he doesn't intervene sooner in a world of rape, corruption and natural disaster. Let's face it, God's footprints are *unseen* to eyes of flesh. So when our spiritual vision strains to discern the outline of his feet ahead, we may wonder whether it's all an illusion. We may wonder if we've misheard the whispers and misinterpreted our encounter with God.

Colliding Worldviews

Human suffering is only one challenge to belief we'll face. Our western world also offers a thriving marketplace of ideas and philosophies to explain our origins, interpret our existence and understand life's ultimate meaning. Doubt can be an inevitable outcome as we explore, trial and attempt to reconcile these different ideas.

For instance, Greg once posted a comment on my website, TheThoughtFactory.net. Having enrolled in university, Greg was experiencing a great deal of doubt about God in light of the evolutionary theory he was being taught. "If the human species evolved from a single cell organism, which science believes to be a fact," Greg explained, "then I do not believe there can be a Creator God – at least not the one I was brought up to believe in. The idea that God created this original life form some 4.5 billion years ago and then watched and waited for humans to appear in his image is too ridiculous to entertain. He surely would have better things to do! I still believe that Jesus was a one-of-a-kind inspirational hero of the time, completely deserving of admiration and celebration. But it seems he could not have had divine origins, or had a miracle resurrection." Greg was encountering the worldview of evolution and finding his spirituality sitting uncomfortably with it.

Greg's experience is by no means isolated. David Tacey, an associate professor in arts at Melbourne's La Trobe University, has seen many of his literature and spirituality students abandon their religious beliefs for a "secular" spirituality of their own. "It is a story often told with enthusiasm and optimism," David says, "as if telling of a movement from bondage to freedom, from darkness to light." And yet he adds, "The secular world constantly tells us that 'religion' is about indoctrination, conditioning and coercion, and therefore must be bad. What it does not tell us is that secularism itself is a potent form of indoctrination, all the more potent for not being detected as such."[1]

In our modern society, a variety of understandings about the world and God are available. But perhaps we've become oblivious to the religion most promoted through our educational and media institutions – secularism. It's a religion intent on distilling the world into formulas containable to human minds and keen on writing God out of life's script.

Either way, those with open minds will experience doubt at some stage as they navigate through a variety of truth claims.

Right now my opinion is, I hope there's an afterlife, but I think this is it. That's why I fear death. Religious people never fear death, only the sadness of losing someone.

US TALK SHOW HOST, LARRY KING[2]

The British Broadcasting Corporation once conducted a poll called *Who Do You Worship?*[3] Run in conjunction with a television series on modern beliefs about God, the survey asked respondents from ten countries two basic questions: Who or what do you worship, and what are the reasons? The responses posted on the BBC's website made great reading. Some worshipped Allah, some worshipped Jesus, a few bowed to Buddha and one person worshipped George Clooney! Some trusted science, some believed in the goodness of humanity, some dismissed God's existence altogether. Every comment was telling and a few were humorous (an American named Matt said, "I worship myself. When you're this good it's hard not to").

Amongst the variety of viewpoints the voice of doubt was heard too. As I read through these comments, I couldn't help wonder how God might reply if the responses were put to him directly. How would God respond to his supporters, his accusers and to others simply bewildered and doubting his reality?

An imaginary conversation began to unfold in my mind.

Sheridan:
OK God, thanks for making time to respond to some of these comments.
Let's start with Kasper in Canada who says you are nothing more than the product of our imagination. "We created God," Kasper says. "One day He will mutate or vanish." You know, I hate it when they talk about you like that.

God: *Well, Kasper's got a point.*

Sheridan: Really?

God: *My name is associated with many imagined deities – you've already mentioned that yourself.*

Sheridan: Like the angry-father god, or the you-must-be-perfect god?

God: *How about the Mercedes-mansions-and-millions god, or the (insert party name) political god? Many create me in their own image.*

Sheridan: But, you're not about to mutate or vanish?

God: *Well, over time some understandings of me will vanish. More people believe in the indulgent-grandfather god today than the resident-policeman god of a few decades ago. But I will be truly found by those who truly search.*

Sheridan: So, maybe even the 'nonexistent god' is just a product of our imagination too?

God: *Think on that for a while and get back to me.*

Sheridan: The next comment is from Ralph in London who says there's no point worshipping you unless you want to be worshipped. And if you're so insecure that you need to be worshipped, then you are not as all-powerful as you're cracked up to be.

God: *Remember that sunset you photographed at Scarborough Beach last year?*

Sheridan: That brilliant red and purple one? That was amazing.

God: *How did you feel watching it?*

Sheridan: Awe-struck. Everyone at the beach did. All we could do was stare at it, then look at each other and utter silly words like 'wow'.

God: *What do you understand worship to be?*

Sheridan: Hey, I thought I was asking you the questions.

(Silence)

Sheridan: Sorry. I remember hearing someone say worship was best described as worth-ship; expressing something as having worth or being valuable.

God: *Am I valuable to you, Sheridan?*

Sheridan: Yes! Absolutely. Immeasurably.

God: *Just like that Scarborough Beach sunset?*

Sheridan: Yes, but even more really.

God: *Why don't you worship a sunset, or your wife, or something else that is valuable and inspires you?*

Sheridan: Well, because you're bigger than them.

God: *Bigger?*

Sheridan: More powerful than all the world's sunsets and wives put together. (Although some wives can be quite powerful…)

God: *Who gave the sunset its colour?*

Sheridan: You.

God: *Who gave women their beauty?*

Sheridan: You. (And I have a couple of other questions on that topic…)

God: *I do not need your worship. I never have. I want a relationship with you – communication. And amongst other things, worship is your expressing to me in word and action why you value me, the painter of sunsets, the originator of beauty, the one greater than all such splendour combined.*

Sheridan: I hope Ralph reads this.

God: *You haven't fully understood worship either. For the moment though, would you like to move on?*

Sheridan: Alright. Johnny from Leicester says, "Life is about knowing God, worshipping our creator, and following his perfect plan for our lives. This is a dynamic path of discovery which can be easily cluttered with man-made 'religious' paraphernalia."

God: *Have you seen the new Jesus action figure yet?*

Sheridan: Yeah, I did. It was advertised right alongside the Jesus T-shirt, pencil case and glow-in-the-dark Frisbee.

God: *They've got a Holy Odour Eater out now too – an insert for your shoe with my name on it.*

Sheridan: Missed that one. Must've been too busy looking at the bobble-head John Calvin, Martin Luther and Mother Teresa dolls.

God: *The church history figurines have always sold well.*

Sheridan: There's a lot of money to be made from you, isn't there.

God: *Billions.*

Sheridan: And, what do you think about that?

God: *One seeks me, another uses me. One day both will meet me face to face.*

Sheridan: Rustan from England says, "Organised religion is for the weak and timid. Why on earth people need to feel…"

God: *Weak and timid?*

Sheridan: Well, that's what he says.

God: *Remember Telemachus?*

Sheridan: Umm, I haven't read the Old Testament in a while…

God: *He's not in the Bible. Telemachus was a priest who lived in the fifth century. On a visit to Rome he visited the Colosseum and saw gladiatorial combat. He was so abhorred by what the men were doing to each other that he stepped into the arena and pleaded with them to stop.*

Sheridan: What happened?

God: *The crowd stoned him.*

Sheridan: Oh.

God: *Honorius – in charge at the time – heard about the event, hailed Telemachus a martyr and put a stop to the sport. Through Telemachus, the bloodthirsty entertainment of the Romans was brought to an end.*

Sheridan: Gutsy.

God: *Obedient.*

Sheridan: Martin Luther King Jnr. lost his life fighting racism. William Wilberforce lost the chance to become British Prime Minister by opposing the slave trade. Both said they were motivated by your call for justice.

God: *Millions have sacrificed all in following me and serving others.*

Sheridan: Sometimes it's not easy to follow you at all.

God: *You cannot serve both me and yourself. Set me as your priority and all your needs will be met beyond expectation.*

Sheridan: Abubakar in Scotland says, "As a Muslim I believe that God is compassionate and merciful. It is really frightening to see people in the West moving deeper into materialism and losing touch with the spiritual side."

God: *If only more people saw what Abubakar sees.*

Sheridan: That we're losing touch with our spiritual sides?

God: *That materialism is a religion in itself. I have no problem with your markets. But your advertising preaches that humans remain incomplete without new fashions and novelties; your shopping centres quickly become temples where the empty flock to find wholeness; your cash registers then become altars on which your offerings are placed. Yet, the more you consume the more unsatisfied you feel.*

Sheridan: On the subject of religion, Elspeth in Montreal is a humanist and believes that religion only divides people and was designed by the wealthy and powerful to keep the poor obedient. I guess you're going to agree with her too?

God: *Partly.*

Sheridan: Which part?

God: *Religion often divides people – in the sense of labelling some as acceptable and others as not. I love all people – the rich, the homeless, the Arab and the Jew. I have never been a fan of religion.*

Sheridan: Oh?

God: *Religion often treats me as though I can be "bought" by performing certain rituals – reciting verses, touching relics, giving money. You cannot earn my favour. I am not an idol.*

Sheridan: So, religion is useless?

God: *The pursuit of religion is a sign of your need. Why else would there be such spiritual questing across all nationalities unless I had put that impulse within you? But religion is not your fulfilment. I am.*

Sheridan: I guess some of the problem lies with certain religious leaders and adherents. Some Christians have done despicable things in your name.

God: *Yes, some have.*

Sheridan: Some – like those child-abusing religious leaders – have destroyed people's lives.

God: (solemnly) *Yes, some have.*

Sheridan: Some – like those people who tell others to get their lives right yet go home and scream at their own wives – well, they're just hypocrites.

God: *Yes, some are.*

Sheridan: Some – like those people with "Jesus loves you" bumper stickers on their cars who go and…

God: *Be careful Sheridan.*

Sheridan: Sorry?

God: *Remember that speeding ticket you got a little while back?*

Sheridan: Um, yes.

God: *And what about that argument with Jeremy the other day. Your anger clouded your ability to listen to him.*

Sheridan: Yes, well he…

God: *Have you always forgiven others who have wronged you, like I commanded?*

Sheridan: I get your point.

God: *My true followers will be characterised by love, but they will not love perfectly all the time.*

Sheridan: But what about those who harm and kill in your name?

God: *Some masquerade as my people for personal gain. I am a God of justice and there will be a reckoning. Yet, my mercy is available to all. Remember what I did for Paul?*

Sheridan: The apostle? The guy in the New Testament who abused and murdered people until he encountered you?

God: *I turn evil around. Cheats and liars need my forgiveness as much as thieves and murderers.*

Sheridan: Sometimes we must really let you down. I hate to think that some of my actions might have put people off you.

God: *Aim for goodness and apologise for your mistakes. But you can never represent me completely. The true seeker of life must search for me personally.*

Sheridan: The next comment is from Lou in the West Midlands.

God: *Ah, Lou. I have plans for him.*

Sheridan: Lou says, "I would love to believe in God and the afterlife. It would make me happier and not fearful of the future. However, if a god really exists then why is the world the way it is? Why is there famine, murder, rape and hatred all across the world? If God does exist then what is all this? Is it punishment? I don't know what to believe." I must admit, Lord, I've wondered the same things from time to time.

God: *So have I.*

Sheridan: Eh?!

God: *I wonder why there is famine in the world when there is enough food to go around. I wonder why some go without clothing or shelter while others live in sprawling homes and bulging walk-in wardrobes. I wonder why thousands die each day from thirst while others complain about the amount of froth on their cappuccino. Why do you hoard your wealth?*

Sheridan: But what about evil dictators and murderers and...

God: *I wonder how humans can fight to protect their personal freedom yet blame me when another uses their freedom for evil. Which would you prefer – to choose your own actions or to be automated?*

Sheridan: But what about natural disasters like floods and earthquakes and tsunamis?

God: *I wonder why pollutants from your manufacturing plants continue to destabilise nature. I wonder why the earth's resources continue to be depleted when better care could be taken of them. When will you look after what I have given you?*

Sheridan: But what about babies born with deformities? What about teenagers with terminal illnesses? What about old men with Alzheimer's disease?

God: *This world is not as I made it. And it breaks my heart. Ever since the first humans chose to disregard my instructions the world has been cursed with brokenness. Yet I am making all things new.*

Sheridan: But you're all-powerful. You could do something now.

God: *Do you think I do not care? Do you think I turn away from the sight of suffering? Do you think I do not groan at every attack on the humanity I created to live with me? What do you suggest I do?*

Sheridan: Stop the evil. Change the world.

God: *The day is coming when all evil will cease, my friend. But when that day comes there will be no chance left to choose. Each one's reward will be given; each person's destiny set. Many are not ready for me to come as their judge. In the meantime, I call you to begin the process of rebuilding the world.*

Sheridan: But, still...

God: *Will you trust me in this?*

I think God wants you to question, because what kind of God would He be if He didn't understand how our mind works? I believe He created us, so He's gotta know how hard it is to live here. So I no longer feel guilty about having questions – I think it's an essential part of this faith.

LEIGH NASH, FROM *SIXPENCE NONE THE RICHER*[4]

[doubt and the seeking heart]

Doubt will most likely rear its head sometime along our journey of faith. But I wonder if God is more interested in the softness and pliability of our heart than our actual crisis of faith itself. Some people doubt God out of an arrogant, scoffing soul. Others sincerely wrestle, looking for their truth with an open spirit.

I once interviewed a prominent member of the Australian Sceptics Society. With me being a committed Christian and my guest a committed sceptic, we knew we wouldn't agree on everything related to the more intangible aspects of the universe. But my guest's information was important to stop people being ripped off by entrepreneurial hucksters ready to prey on people searching for hope. We had a wonderful time exploring the exaggerated claims behind things like crop circles, spoon bending, walking on hot coals and bogus psychic readings.

My interest was piqued by my interviewee's questioning, investigative mind and I wanted to know if spirituality was off the menu for her all together. The conversation continued something like this:

Sheridan: Does being a sceptic rule out a spiritual world for you altogether?

Guest: No, it doesn't. It gets down to your definition of spirituality, which is something we can question forever. But my spirituality is based around the awesome nature of reality. I don't think we need psychics and spontaneous human combustion to really be astounded by what's out there. Chaos Theory basically says that the world is so complex you can never predict or define it totally with equations. It's that complexity in reality which I find inspirational. Where it comes from becomes a theological question which I don't think I'm qualified to answer, and I'm still on that search.

Sheridan: I know there have been doctors who have gotten interested in God after entering medical school. When they saw the order of the human body they said 'this is so well designed, there must be some genius behind it.'

Guest: I can see that argument. I don't know what it is but the level of design that comes out in Chaos Theory and Fractal Geometry is just stunningly beautiful. I've got a lot of problems searching this area in that I cannot find answers for the suffering that's in the world. For me, reincarnation looked like a very good answer but unfortunately I need more evidence to believe it. I would love to be able to understand all those questions and I can't. I haven't managed to get tangible evidence that's got me there yet. But I've got a good few years yet to keep searching.

My guest was a doubter, but not a scoffer; a sceptic, but one searching. If she keeps up an honest heart-felt search I wonder how long it will take before she bumps into the one who says, *I will be found when you seek me with all your heart.*[5]

It's interesting to see the way Jesus responded to doubters during his earthly visit. When his cousin John doubted whether he really was the prophet the world had been waiting for, Jesus encouraged his relative to consider the miracles he was performing and the lives he was touching.[6] When Jesus' friend Thomas couldn't believe that he had come back to life after crucifixion, Jesus appeared to him and invited Thomas to touch his wounds, to stop doubting and believe.[7] Jesus responded personally to those experiencing doubt, even when they should've known better.[8] The only doubters he had little time for were the religious leaders of the day, who scoffed in proud arrogance at the spiritual light he was bringing.

"There are only three types of people," said the seventeenth century mathematician and philosopher Blaise Pascal: "those who have found God and serve him; those who have not found God and seek him, and those who live not seeking or finding him." Pascal observed the first as rational and happy, the second as rational and unhappy, and the third as both unhappy and foolish. I'm sure God looks in love at all three groups, but I wonder if he smiles most on the first two. Wandering through the heartland of doubt, seekers walk with eyes open asking for directions, while the proud sit reading their comic books.

In faith there is enough light for those who want to believe and enough shadows to blind those who don't.

BLAISE PASCAL

[doubt's invitation]

Doubt can be a frightening experience. When long-held beliefs begin to tremble and sway it can feel like the ground beneath our feet is crumbling; like the staircases we were climbing in life have turned to sand.

But there is an optimistic side to such crises of faith. Doubt separates old beliefs from new. It is the passageway to a new door of understanding. In a culture of instant ease and drive-thru belief, doubt invites us to check our assumptions, assertions and persuasions and ensure our lives are built on something stable. Is our faith based on dry academics, borrowed facts alone? Or does it rest on flimsy emotional reaction, a past thrill or shiver? Doubt calls us to marry intellect and emotion by knowing God more. It invites us to engage our faith and face our questions, to explore its sacred text and mine its treasures, and to examine the lives of a multitude who have walked the path before us and found it firm.

"Now that I'm a Christian I do have moods in which the whole thing looks very improbable," wrote CS Lewis two decades after his divine encounter. He then added "but when I was an atheist I had moods in which Christianity looked entirely probable." Lewis discovered that true faith needed to be grounded on more than fluctuant moods, sensing that "unless you teach your moods 'where they get off', you can never be either a sound Christian or even a sound atheist, but just a creature dithering to and from, with its beliefs really dependent on the weather and the state of its digestion."[9]

There may be times when we wonder if this dance with God is nothing more than an animated fairytale projected on the interior wall of our souls. But doubt beckons us out of ourselves and deeper into the heart of God. It invites us to discover the divine-human conversation that is Prayer, the sacred recording of divine movements through history that is the Bible, the company of fellow journeyers that is the Faith Community.

To the open-hearted, doubt can be the groomsman holding the ring to the beloved.

A guide ushering us towards deeper intimacy with God.

There are two ways to slide easily through life; to believe everything or to doubt everything. Both ways save us from thinking.

AUTHOR, LOGICIAN, & SCIENTIST, ALFRED KORZYBSKI

God: *Sheridan?*

Sheridan: Oh, I thought we'd finished.

God: *The conversation is never finished. Did you want it to?*

Sheridan: No, I... I quite enjoyed it.

God: *Remember your moment of doubt?*

Sheridan: Which one?

God: *The big one.*

Sheridan: Oh, you mean when I was at Bible College? When I read all those academics' views and got all confused? That was horrible.

God: *Why was it horrible?*

Sheridan: Because I started to seriously doubt whether you existed. I mean, it seemed like all these scholars had so many different, often contradictory views about you. I began wondering whether any of us could really know anything about you for sure. I wondered whether I'd given my life to a lie.

God: *I remember your confusion well.*

Sheridan: Well, you seemed pretty distant at the time. Others talked about how you were answering their prayers in miraculous ways. I just felt abandoned.

God: *Did you feel abandoned that night by the Brisbane River?*

Sheridan: No... that was very special indeed.

God: *Go on.*

The night by the Brisbane River

When the flame of faith was first lit within me I enjoyed three warm years of God's presence in my life. That divine encounter had changed my course of direction. In the early days of this new companionship I wasn't yet sure what God had in store for me (I never imagined I'd be doing what I do now), but I knew that God was leading me along a new pathway. It was scary and exciting all at once – the way following the unseen footprints of God is meant to be.

After a series of unexplainable coincidences following prayer, I was sure God was first taking me to the front steps of academic study. Having become captured by the depth and power of the Bible's message, it seemed I was to spend time delving into its narratives, poetry, lyrics and wisdom. Now, I wasn't too inclined towards text books and seminars. But little did I know that God would set in motion a hunger to explore life and meaning through that experience.

So I enrolled in my Bible College degree and began to read and reflect and listen and study. My shelves began filling up with books and my mind began filling up with theories.

And, slowly, my heart began filling up with doubts.

I was studying in a fine, faith-filled environment with students and staff who'd encountered God too. But a good study program will expose you to views you've never considered, even arguments you downright reject. To not engage with these ideas is to weave ourselves into a cocoon. It was through examining differing viewpoints that I began to get confused and witness the gradual diminishing of that flame within.

I read the theologians' books and faith got murky. Some believed the Bible was historically accurate, others said it was a bunch of fairytales. Some said the resurrection of Jesus was a fable, others said the evidence was undeniable. Why some academics who don't believe in God would want to dedicate so much time to writing about him is a mystery to me. But were they right? My season of doubt had begun. It would last several months.

One early evening I ventured down to a favourite spot – a table in parklands running alongside the Brisbane River. To this bench I brought a notebook, a Bible, a Chocolate-Strawberry milkshake (the kind I often get when feeling low), and my cloud-covered soul. God had seemed so close. Now he seemed so distant. Had it all been an illusion? I had to find God again, if he was there to be found.

The Choc-Strawberry milkshake hadn't lasted long, or helped all that much. With the last few drops turning warm at the bottom of the cup I reached for my Bible. I had been crying out to God for clarity, yet so far my prayers had seemed to go ignored. Would anything be different now? I opened my worn copy of Holy Scripture. It happened to fall to the 77th Psalm. I began to read:

> I cried out to God for help;
> I cried out to God to hear me.
> When I was in distress, I sought the Lord;
> at night I stretched out untiring hands
> and my soul refused to be comforted.

That's me, I thought to myself. That's… me. I found such honesty strangely comforting. I read on.

> I remembered you, O God, and I groaned;
> I mused, and my spirit grew faint.
> You kept my eyes from closing;
> I was too troubled to speak.
> I thought about the former days,
> the years of long ago;
> I remembered my songs in the night…

I had been experiencing insomnia for months now. I was weary. Even thinking about God brought a kind of sorrow to me. But it seemed I was not alone. Someone had walked a similar road of "songs in the night" that could no longer be sung.

> Will the Lord reject forever?
> Has his unfailing love vanished forever?
> Has God forgotten to be merciful?

Reading such words was startling. I knew the Bible talked about prayer. I knew the Bible talked about trusting God. But I had never known that it talked about doubt and dark nights of the soul – the kind of experiences I was in the midst of. It was as if Someone had reached over my shoulder and opened my Bible to this very page...

> I will remember the deeds of the LORD;
> yes, I will remember your miracles of long ago.
> I will meditate on all your works
> and consider all your mighty deeds.

By now I felt as if a warm hand had touched my back and was directing me forward. I pulled out my notebook and my cap-less supermarket pen and started scribbling. I began to recall those "miracles of long ago", moments when I'd *known* that I'd known that God had been there. I remembered serendipitous moments in response to prayer, astounding "coincidences" that had led me further into joy. I thought of the world's design and order, and the existence of beauty and love. I thought about the Bible's amazing continuity of message, a miracle given its being written across three millennia by a multitude of writers. I began to remember the emptiness and futility I'd faced before my divine encounter. And I remembered a God who visited a planet, a planet that had crucified him, and a love that still welcomed that planet back to himself. After an hour of writing I could feel a small flicker of warmth within.

> What god is so great as our God?
> You are the God who performs miracles;
> you display your power among the peoples.
> With your mighty arm you redeemed your people…

I knew from my studies that Asaph, the writer of Psalm 77, was here alluding to the greatest event in ancient Jewish history – The Exodus. After the Israelites had spent 400 years in slavery to Egyptians, a guy called Moses had been directed by God to lead them to freedom. When their journey required crossing the Red Sea to escape their trailing captors, God had parted the waters, allowing the people to walk across its dry bed. If you've seen the Cecil B deMille classic *The Ten Commandments*, you've got an idea as to what went on. Asaph remembered such a landmark event in his people's faith and concluded:

> Your path led through the sea,
> your way through the mighty waters,
> though your footprints were not seen.

I don't recall how long I sat at that bench, jotting experiences in that notebook, working out those doubts. Time seemed to compress. The parklands were dark now and moths flew around the street light near my table. But in those few hours I had experienced another encounter with the divine. I had been reminded that God's footprints have always been unseen. But like the force of a wind gust, the sound of a voice or the warmth of a flame, unseen does not equal unreal. As I got up from the park bench, threw my milkshake cup into the bin nearby and walked slowly into the cool night air, a flame was again burning in my spirit. Somehow I was meant to turn to that Psalm. Through an unexpected meeting with an unfamiliar verse I'd tasted again the infinite love of an unfathomable God.

And since that moment I've learnt that a tested faith, a faith stretched by the forces of doubt, can rebound richer and more resilient than before.

Why?

God: *Because I draw close to those who stay close to me through their crisis of belief.*

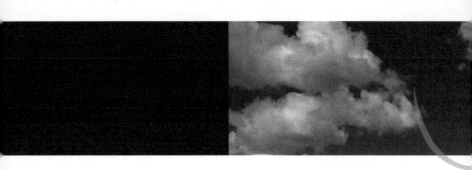

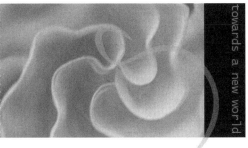

>>> **CHAPTER SIX**
DREAM: TOWARDS
A NEW WORLD

There's something about plane travel that always excites me.

Okay, even the best string of in-flight movies can't save the really long trips. And I find unusual cravings develop after consuming those little trays of food – appetites for hideous things like carrot juice and detox diets. But nothing beats that thrust down the tarmac and the ascension from earth to sky. Climbing toward the clouds my eyes are opened to a grander view than is normally available. I always take my journal with me on plane flights. On descent it's often filled with fresh thoughts, insights and aspirations.

The world looks different from the heavenly perspective. Roads that looked straight from the ground are found to kink and wriggle like straightened out farm wire. Untravelled paths reveal their final destinations with tracks leading to new townships and others leading to dead ends. Where allotments of land seemed square the big picture proves them oblong. Where hills once hid valleys all is exposed. We see forest edges; their expansion and their limits. We see properties and boundaries; where responsibility begins and ends.

Crossing rural outskirts we see green fields resting by the dry and thirsty; areas of growth and corners of neglect. We see how lines left by a busy tractor make coherent themes and designs in the paddock. Up high we see connections between things previously unrelated; we find alternative routes we never knew existed; we discover how each small part interconnects to form the whole.

As we rise above the buildings and cities that usually mask the horizon we soon begin losing sight of earth itself. Climbing to ten, twenty, then thirty thousand feet we break through to another world – a kingdom above the clouds, above earthly storms and turbulence; a world that is bright, white, and flooded with the warm unfiltered light of the sun. And from there the world takes on new meaning.

Yes, the world looks different from the heavenly perspective.

Don't let us love the road rather than the land to which it leads, lest we lose our homeland altogether.

CELTIC SAINT, COLUMBANUS

As we continue pursuing his footsteps, God leads us to such a high point. We follow him and find ourselves looking at life from a new perspective. Standing by our side, God begins pointing out aspects of our world we'd never quite seen before.

He begins with small things – the intricate design of a leaf, the intelligence behind a piece of architecture, an act of kindness performed for a stranger. Viewed from the heavenly perspective everyday things like these seem to take on new meaning. God points out a parent's smile at their child's football goal, a couple of friends talking deeply across a café table, an elderly couple in cardigans walking their Jack Russell together. Such things are now viewed with more beauty and reverence. And from this vantage point we can see small flickers of flame lighting up in the souls of others beginning to encounter the divine along their life journey.

But the world is not some lavender-scented basket full of petals and smiles and saccharine-sounding birthday cards. God begins showing us the broken parts too – a world where a child dies from hunger and curable disease nearly every three seconds; where over 8,000 people die from AIDS and another 14,000 contract HIV everyday; where an estimated 246 million children are engaged in child labour, and where over a billion people live on less than $1 a day. God points to the one billion people living in slums, to the one billion lacking access to clean water, to the 2.6 billion lacking toilets and other forms of sanitation. He points to a sombre couple walking from the divorce court, an addict passed out in an alleyway, a multitude searching for purpose, guidance, liberation and belonging. He points out those with no flicker in their souls yet.

Then God turns to us. He recounts our journey so far and some monumental moments along the way. We laugh at the childhood pranks, wince at the grazed knees, recall the early dreams, laugh again at the attempts to fly like a superhero. God affirms the talents we have, our unique strengths, flairs and passions. Then with gentle but firm words he highlights areas in our lives needing attention – relationships that have become dry through neglect; thorny attitudes about colleagues and relatives; pride and conceit, perhaps even outright deceit; occasional greed maybe. With each of our apologies comes a forgiving smile and a warm wave of freedom within.

Follow me to the end, he says, looking deep into our eyes. *I want to lead you to a new world.*

And then he begins to share his dream with us.

[the dream of God]

God is leading us somewhere. His footprints do not walk in circles – there is a destination. God has a dream, a vision, a future reality that he is ushering all history toward. God's unseen footprints are leading us to a new world – a world called heaven.

Now, heaven is an interesting concept. For many, the word brings to mind white-gowned spirits sitting on clouds, strumming harps and singing the Hallelujah Chorus all day, every day, for all eternity. For years I wondered if I really wanted to live in a place like that! But gradually I came to understand that my vision of heaven was more informed by comic strips and popular myth than from sacred Scripture. When I delved into my copy of the Bible I discovered a vision of heaven quite different to all that.

As I read these biblical descriptions of heaven[1] I discovered a place I wanted to be part of. Instead of clouds I found a new land; instead of individual floating souls I found a new community; instead of some ethereal existence I found a place encompassing the everyday hopes of humankind.

Heaven, I discovered, is a new world living under God's rule. You could use the classical word "kingdom" to describe it. And with God at its centre, the Bible describes heaven as a place flooded with light. Heaven as a Kingdom of Light – I can just imagine it...

In the Kingdom of Light the seeking heart finds its home. The unseen footprints have led to its city steps and not even death has stopped our entering in. This land is the pilgrim's destination and reward, yet is itself a new challenge and a fresh journey. All is new in the Kingdom of Light, but not in the novel sense of "new". It has all the grace of an eighteenth century theatre or the most established of parks with the oldest of trees, yet everything is strong, healthy, alive.

The Kingdom of Light is a place of plenty. No one hoards and no one goes without. No one shivers and all have homes. There is ownership of possessions but no materialism, enjoyment of goods but no consumerism, individuality without narcissism. Citizens of the Kingdom share their belongings out of freedom, generosity and joy, not guilt, debt or coercion. The greatest happiness is found in another's delight.

In the Kingdom of Light there is a balance of life never before experienced. There are community-wide celebrations and moments of individual solitude. There is time for vigorous labour and time for creative expression. There is elation and rest, play and thought. There are undeserved gifts and effort-earned rewards. This is a safe place for privacy and a safe place to be known. This is a place of equilibrium.

Work is meaningful in the Kingdom of Light. Each job has significance, each task its special place. Effort is satisfying, exertion rewarding, sleep is deep. Each member contributes according to their God-given design. The writer finds his inspiration, the landscaper works her earth. The philosopher discovers her meaning then finds another (and another) idea to ponder. The chef seasons and sautés then finds his dishes improve even more next time around.

The Hebrew greeting *shalom* resonates throughout the Kingdom, and with good reason. The land is indeed a place of "total peace and complete wholeness". The Kingdom is whole. Its environment is whole. The people are whole. Their relationships are whole. Scars of mind are healed, wounds of body are made right. Jealousy has been replaced with honour as each member celebrates the other's success. Swords have been hammered into trowels since conflict and death has made way for cultivation and life.

Right in the centre of the Kingdom stands a giant dining hall housing the largest banquet table imaginable. To this table come the King's companions, all holding their personal invitations. Place names hardly reveal the variety amongst the chosen. Only as the guests arrive is it apparent that this a place for all. Arab, Asian, Tutsi, Aboriginal – no nationality is missed, no tribe has been forgotten. The radical sits next to the timid, the shy beside the extrovert. An artist sits next to an engineer, a union worker alongside an executive. A one-time vagrant strides up to aristocracy, a mother breaks bread with a rock star. Not that titles really matter anymore. Members of this new community no longer define themselves by the demographics of occupation and income, or the status symbols of label and brand name. They are simply guests, friends – children even – of the King.

And the King… well, words fail to describe him. He shines brighter than the sun. His radiance lights the entire land, yet the brilliance is warm and approachable, not hot and destructive. As he shimmers with every colour the citizens can hardly look anywhere else. Stepping down from his throne the King welcomes each person into the Kingdom, calming any anxiety left from the old world and wiping away any residual tear. And his face! They have followed his footsteps for so long, but now they finally see his face. It is a strong face. Kind. He smiles. They see his lips and hear his voice clearly; there are no whispers anymore. And the King's first words are never forgotten: *Well done, faithful follower! Come in and share my happiness.*

And the Kingdom of Light shares the life and company of its King, in an ever-present now.

And the Kingdom's citizens forever honour the One who has made them fully alive.

There are moments when I stop working, turn my gaze to the sunlit world outside my study window, and wonder just what living in that heavenly Kingdom will be like. So far I've had a pretty enjoyable thirty-three years of life on this planet, but there is pain and disappointment I can't wait to see dissolved in the warm light of that new world. I wonder what my life will be like without insomnia, something I constantly wrestle with. I wonder how Dave, a friend of mine, will look when his schizophrenia is gone and he has peace of mind. I wonder what my mother will say the moment her various illnesses drop away from her body. I wonder what relationships will be like without miscommunication, selfishness or fear complicating them. (I also wonder what members of the police, fire and ambulance services will do for a living when there is no more crime, disaster or injury to attend to.)

Fortune tellers try and prophesy the twists and turns of life ahead. Business analysts plot their graphs to predict the market trends of tomorrow. God, instead, gives us his vision of the future – a heavenly Kingdom of Light. It's a vision more secure than uncertain predictions and much larger than any collection of trends. The dream is more than a giddy wish and greater than some utopian hope awaiting its revolution. Heaven is something only God can create, and it's coming. And as another flame flickers to life within another heart, another citizen is added to the Kingdom's resident list. And as each day of history passes by, God's new creation creeps another day closer in fulfilment.

I would give all the wealth of the world, and all the deeds of all the heroes, for one true vision.

ESSAYIST AND POET, HENRY DAVID THOREAU

[people of light]

God has a dream for the world – a vision so blindingly bright that words are inadequate in describing just what it will fully be. But God has a dream for us too. God dreams that we become all he designed us to be, with all our individual flair and talent realized. But he wants even more for us. He dreams of us embodying the luminous character of Jesus Christ, "our lives gradually becoming brighter and more beautiful as God enters our lives and we become like him."[2] God dreams of that flame of faith within us growing until we become people of light.

The Kingdom of Light is a future event. A look at our world quickly reminds us that heaven is not yet here. But we're not to idly wait until the new world dawns. When Jesus paid the earth a bodily visit all those years ago he said the Kingdom's construction had already begun.[3] As he healed the crippled, fed the hungry, touched the unloved and embraced the outcasts, Jesus was demonstrating the values and power of that new land. With each step he walked and each word he spoke, light from the future world broke onto the earth. Jesus began changing the world that is, into the world that will one day be.

And he calls his followers to do the same.

God leads us to the high point, shares with us his grand vision and extends to us an invitation – to be his people, citizens of the coming Kingdom, transforming this world into the light-drenched land of God:

> Imitating the generosity of God by sharing our wealth, feeding the hungry, housing the poor.

> Expressing the life of God by protecting the vulnerable, healing the broken, working for peace.

● Cultivating the heart of God by blessing those who curse, forgiving those who betray, embracing the ridiculed and rejected.

● Celebrating the love of God by inviting others to the banquet table, to the Kingdom of Light, to the Jesus who forgives and embraces and transforms.

For a generation longing to find its purpose, to a generation looking for a cause to live, Jesus extends an invitation – to embrace his dream and collaborate in shaping the world that is, into the world that will one day be.

The place God calls you to is
where your deep gladness and
the world's deep hunger meet.

AUTHOR, FREDERICK BUECHNER[4]

I have seen the power and values of heaven touch and change our world. Whether it's a former brothel madam encountering God and deciding to run a refuge for girls coming off the street, or an entrepreneur training poor business owners to grow their ventures and employ others, followers of Christ are working to make this world more like the world to come. And God is often performing miracles in the process.

I remember meeting Julian for the first time at a church in Perth, Western Australia. I was speaking from the platform and Julian was sitting in one of the front rows. He had recently encountered God, had been brought to church by a friend, and because he wasn't yet familiar with typical church 'protocol', continued interrupting me with his questions. Julian had some great thoughts and I'm glad he ignored his friend's encouragement to sit quietly like everyone else. Over the next few months I really enjoyed talking with Julian and exploring some of his questions about God and Christian life. Sometimes I'd see him crying in church, simply thankful for what Christ was doing in his life.

Julian was an attractive man with styled black hair and a ballroom dancer's build. Yet his face was often pale, a little sunken, and at times he looked too thin. And we discovered the reason. Julian was Human Immunodeficiency Virus-positive – he had AIDS. During an operation to remove a collapsed lung, Julian had acquired the virus from a transfusion of contaminated blood. His white blood cells were now being destroyed, making his immune system weak and leaving Julian open to sickness and ultimately death.

Julian rang me one day. "I've come across this bit in the Bible," he said. "Can I read it to you?" He flicked open to the page and read from the book of James:

Is any one of you sick? He should call the elders of the church to pray over him and anoint him with oil in the name of the Lord. And the prayer offered in faith will make the sick person well; the Lord will raise him up. If he has sinned, he will be forgiven. Therefore confess your sins to each other and pray for each other so that you may be healed.[5]

"So," he said, returning to me, "what do you think about that?"

"I think we need to make some phone calls!" I replied. I called around the leaders of the church and arranged a time for us to pray for Julian's healing.

Later that week we gathered in a small room in the church complex. We had the oil ready – a symbol of God's Spirit who heals. We had the leaders ready – as we were directed to. We sat Julian in a seat and, along with some of his close friends, gathered around and placed our hands on his shoulders. In the privacy of this confidential group, Julian confessed to God the sins of his past. Then each of us took turns in asking God to heal our friend. Finally, oil was placed on Julian's forehead and the senior pastor of the church said, "Julian, be healed in the name of Jesus." There was a great sense of anticipation in the room. It felt like a divine moment.

Well, it's always a risk praying like that. You're never quite sure what God will do as, ultimately, miracles are up to him.[6] But it was with some expectation that Julian went for his next round of monthly blood tests.

The results came back. Julian's white blood cells had decreased even further. He was getting worse, not better.

The following month's tests also gave little encouragement. This time the white blood cells hadn't dropped any further, but they hadn't increased either. There was more prayer in church and at home with friends. But we wondered whether God had already given us his answer.

Then Julian went for his next round of tests, the third after that original prayer meeting. The doctor looked incredulously at the printed report and said some sort of mistake must have happened during the procedure. He arranged for another blood test to double-check. But those results came back the same. The virus was no longer evident in Julian's body. His white blood cell count was normal. There was now no trace of HIV whatsoever in Julian's system.

Julian had been healed of AIDS.

I lost touch with Julian for a while and then, about a year later, a hand touched my shoulder as I sat in a coffee shop. I turned around and hardly recognised the person behind me. It was Julian, but where his face had once looked sunken and pale, his complexion and features were now full, healthy and tanned. The healing had stayed. And the doctors were still amazed.

Heaven is not yet with us, that's for certain. But in the meantime God is changing this world to make it more like the new world that's coming. Through miracles like Julian's, we glimpse that future place where "scars of mind are healed and wounds of body are made right." And as I discovered anew through Julian's experience, God calls his followers to be part of the action.

A High Calling

So, God calls us to become part of his mission of world transformation – praying and serving toward his dream. Along the way he'll do the miraculous, but a good deal of the time it will be simply hard work. God's invitation to follow is a high calling indeed.

Our culture can be like a conveyor belt ride; we are offered an easy trip by stepping on, and as it glides us through its malls and offices we are invited to consume and compete like everyone else. In contrast, the pathway of Christ is narrow, at times rocky, and demands counter-cultural ethics and lifestyle. Accepting the call to follow those unseen footprints to the end means accepting an invitation to change.

Following Christ means a change of heart. The journey results in a transformation of thought, will and emotion. Following Christ shapes our attitudes, beliefs and behaviour and influences our relationships, dating patterns and treatment of others. It reforms our use of money, our purchasing habits and the quantity of our possessions, and challenges our career decisions, our response to injustice and the amount of food we eat. It changes the way we express disappointment, resolve disagreements and respond to mistreatment. With Christ close by, our political ideals, our use of the environment and our care for the rest of his creation changes. Our ethics are realigned and our worldview is revised. The art we produce, the sport we play, the media we consume, the dreams we hold – all are turned upside down as conversion takes place along that narrow path. There will be pain and discomfort, so no wonder the English writer GK Chesterton once remarked, "The Christian ideal has not been tried and found wanting; it has been found difficult and left untried."

God Within

But just when it sounds like all this change is up to us, that it's all about God pointing out the needed adjustments in our lives and world and us trudging off to fix them, we're put straight. As intelligent as humans can be, we will rarely shape this world in ways that will truly last. As beneficial as self-help books and courses can be, human effort alone will never produce the inner transformation God is looking for. So, God offers to empower us himself. He offers to enter our souls and come live and breathe within us.

God does this by giving us his Spirit. "It stands to reason, doesn't it," reflected Saint Paul on this, "that if the alive and present God who raised Jesus from the dead moves into your life, he'll do the same thing in you that he did in Jesus, bringing you alive to himself?"[7] That's what the Spirit does – he creates life. He gives us the energy to change and develop the life of Christ within. Once welcomed, he will fill our souls with love, peace, generosity and goodness. In the future, God's Spirit will even breathe new life into our dead bodies, raising us to an immortal existence in the Kingdom of Light.

History has been changed through everyday people empowered by God's Spirit and willing to accept this high calling. In May 1846, a guest speaker named James Caughey visited a little church in Nottingham. The Bible verse he chose to speak on that night was a promise of Jesus found in the book of Mark: *I tell you, whatever you ask for in prayer, believe that you have received it and it will be yours.*[8] Caughey explained that the key to understanding this promise was to learn to desire what God desires. Caughey added that God's greatest desire was that we develop the character of a servant, to help the poor, and to tell others about Jesus. One particular young guy was sitting in the audience. He'd encountered God two years before but had been drifting in his faith. Then on that May evening God spoke to him.

With the speaker's words burning in his heart, the Spirit of God gave the man a passion to serve others. He acted on this divine direction and devoted himself to starting an organisation committed to telling others about Christ and to serving the needy. That young guy was William Booth and the movement he founded was the Salvation Army. Today, millions of the physically and spiritually hungry across the globe benefit from William Booth's legacy of obedience.

I guess you could call him a saint. William Booth, however, would've probably said that in God's strength he was just helping to make this world a little like the Kingdom to come.

Without exception, I have found that every person who was sincerely happy, radiantly alive, was living for a purpose or a cause beyond himself.

PSYCHOLOGIST, ABRAHAM MASLOW

God takes us to a high point and shows us our world as he sees it – a broken planet that is a caricature of the one he originally created. He then describes the world that will one day be – a Kingdom of Light that endures forever. And he invites us to follow him and live between these two visions; changing the world that is, while awaiting the heaven to come.

At this point in our pursuit of the divine we discover that the journey has a destination – if we choose to complete it. If we take the narrow path of Christ we can expect to be changed along the way. Then one day we will reach our final destination, walk through heaven's gates, and be completely transformed into the people of light God plans for us to be.

"A new world is not made simply by trying to forget the old," wrote the late author Henry Miller. "A new world is made with a new spirit, with new values. Our world may have begun that way, but today it is caricature. Our world is a world of things."

Thankfully, a new world with its new spirit and values is coming.

Yes, things look different from the heavenly perspective.

>>> **CHAPTER SEVEN**

SURRENDER:
SEEING THE
DIVINE ALONG THE
JOURNEY OF LIFE

Art critic Robert Cumming was studying a painting in the London

National Gallery one day. The fifteenth century depiction
of Mary holding the infant Jesus on her lap had been
questioned by critics before, and it was bothering him
now. While there was no doubt that the artist, Filippino
Lippi, was skilful in his use of colour and form, it was the
painter's sense of perspective that had raised eyebrows from
the experts. Hills in the background seemed overly large
and exaggerated, and saints Dominic and Jerome looked
awkward as they knelt before the Christ child. The piece may
have been a classic from the easel of a Renaissance master,
but its proportions seemed all wrong.

As Robert Cumming stood reflecting on the piece, a thought
came to him. Perhaps the problem wasn't so much Filippino
Lippi's, but his own. The painting had never been created to
hang in a gallery. Rather, Lippi had been commissioned to
produce the work as an altarpiece, to be viewed in a place
of prayer. The art critic suddenly realised what he needed to
do. And although feeling a little self-conscious doing it in a
public setting, he obeyed his hunch.

He got down on his knees and knelt before the painting.

Looking up from that reverent posture, Robert Cumming
saw a very different canvas. Mountains that had before
seemed foreboding now eased into place. Saints Dominic
and Jerome now appeared more settled, and Mary seemed
to peer directly into the eyes of the viewer. From a position
of humility Robert Cumming saw what others had missed.
On bended knee the once troubling picture fell into perfect
proportion.[1]

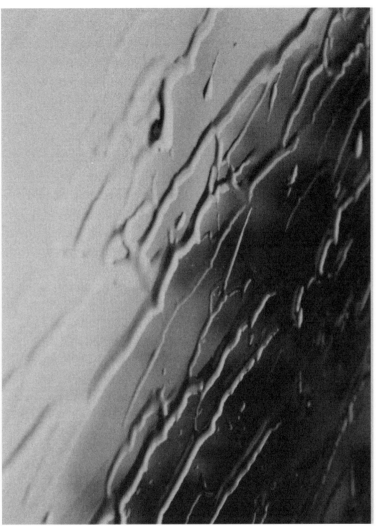

You're blessed when you get your
inside world – your mind and
heart – put right. Then you can see
God in the outside world.

JESUS[2]

[to kneel is to see]

Life can get confusing. At least it can for my generation. On the one hand we chant that popular mantra "do whatever you feel", but on the other we yearn for leaders who will surrender personal gain for the benefit of others. We've listened to university professors claim that no universal truth exists – that we should live by our own individual moral codes. And yet we watch in horror at human rights violations, or the abuse of animals – actions which seem universally wrong. In the middle of such contradictions life can seem confusing and unbalanced, like an initial glance at that Filippino Lippi painting. Yet, as Robert Cumming discovered, perhaps the problem lies not with the picture before us but with ourselves.

I once picked up a newspaper supplement that turned out to be one long advertisement for food and lifestyle products. The front page headline was catchy. In large letters it shouted, "Your body is a temple – worship it!" When we resort to self-worship – the belief that we of all are most important – we stand before life and demand that it suit us. And when millions of people enthrone themselves as supreme, well, life is bound to get confusing.

Robert Cumming's experience hints at another way. When the art critic gave up his pride and knelt down, that confusing picture fell into perspective. Maybe it is only when we stop standing as an authority and begin kneeling in humility that we start to see life correctly and the confusion within dissipates.

So far we've felt the longings, heard the whispers, and even discovered God in the face of Jesus along our journey. We've followed God's lead, climbed to the highpoint and heard his dream for the future. He's described the world-changing mission ahead of us and explained the cost of following him from this point forward. Now God looks at us kindly but firmly, and calls us to make a decision.

Do you wish to see? he asks. *Do you wish to see life clearly, to see the Kingdom of Light, to see me? Then you must relinquish your pride, and kneel. Only I know the terrain ahead. Only I can get you to the destination. Will you return ownership of your life to me?*

Will you surrender?

You see, I believe God has a big picture for every person's life. Unfortunately, most people just live in a b-grade movie of their own creation.

LANDSCAPE PHOTOGRAPHER, KEN DUNCAN

[releasing the future]

It's a scary thing to surrender control of your life to someone.
From a young age most of us have been taught to take control
of our lives, to make our own way, to master our own destinies.
So when God asks us to surrender to him, to release the reins of
the go-cart as we charge down the hill, even the most carefree
experience some fear. We fear that in doing so, we may smack
into someone's letterbox and mess everything up. But some
have taken the risk and found God steering them into the most
unexpected of futures.

There's this great story in the New Testament about Peter, one
of the first followers of Jesus. Peter's profession was fishing and
he ran a little business with his brother Andrew and a couple of
partners, James and John. One morning after a long, exhausting
and ultimately unsuccessful night's work, Peter and his mates
were looking over their fishing nets. As they cleaned, stretched
and mended the nets on shore (probably thinking about warm
baths, hot breakfasts and comfortable beds), Jesus walked up to
Peter and asked for some help.

Wherever Jesus went crowds flocked to hear him speak. Even
on an early morning like this, locals had found him by the
Sea of Galilee and were urging him to teach. Because so many
were pushing towards the lake's edge, Jesus stepped into the
boat belonging to Peter and Andrew and they pushed out a
few metres into the water. When all could see and hear him,
Jesus gave the spiritual lessons the people so wanted. When he
finished, Jesus sat down on the bench and looked at Peter.

Since we're out here, Jesus said, *head into the deeper water and drop the
nets for a catch.*

Peter hadn't heard anything so naïve in a long time and barely
stifled a snigger. Deep water fishing was done at night when the
fish weren't dazzled by the sun's reflection off the water.

Besides, they'd already worked all night without results – the fish just weren't biting – and they'd washed and packed their nets away. The tired and hungry Peter kind of wished Jesus would stick to his religious calling. Fishing was *Peter's* profession. He didn't need advice for something in which he was an authority.

"Well, ah, Master," Peter replied, "we've actually been working the lake hard all night. But if you want to, we'll give it a go."

Peter and Andrew rowed further out and dropped the nets, probably more to pacify their guest than out of any real hope of success. Within moments though, they felt the boat being tugged. Peter pulled on his net and felt weight. Andrew felt pressure on his too. They hauled the nets up and hundreds of fish poured leaping and wriggling into the boat. The same thing happened on the next set of nets, and the next; so many fish that their nets began to break. Peter and Andrew called out to James and John and before long both boats were almost sinking under the miraculous catch of fish.

This was a turning point for Peter. Forgetting the perilous nature of his nearly submerged boat, he threw himself towards Jesus, kneeling in front of him.

"Master, leave. I'm a proud, sinful man and your purity is too much to take."

Don't be afraid, Peter, Jesus replied. *I've got work for you to do. Follow me.*

Peter had met Jesus before; had even seen him heal his mother-in-law.[3] Peter had begun to follow Jesus, but only from a comfortable distance.

Now the call had been given: *I've got work for you to do. Follow me.* Enjoying the teaching and admiring the miracles was one thing. But this was a call to surrender control of his future – his career, his destiny – to Jesus Christ. Would Peter do it?

The story finishes simply:

'They pulled their boats up on shore, left everything and followed him.'[4]

Peter and his friends left their lives by the shoreline to follow Jesus. They walked away from their boats, their identity as fishermen, from their financial security and business plans. Peter knelt, then followed, and had his eyes opened to a new life of adventure and miracle.

What might surrendering our future to God entail? Like Peter and company, it may mean a change of career path. Then again, it might not. It may mean changes to relationships, living arrangements, lifestyle choices. Then again, God may not want these changed at all. God tends to provide the details of such adjustments once we've knelt to him. What surrender entails for sure is a radical reversal of allegiance. We are no longer the final authorities on our lives. Jesus Christ is. He may call for some difficult changes, yes. But could he also lead us to a future we've never dreamt of? Perhaps our dreams are much smaller than his.

[resolving the past]

The future is only one dimension of our lives God wants us to surrender. We have a past as well. And to move into the bright new life of God we must face our failings, acknowledge our wrongs, and surrender them to redeeming hands.

I must share the story of Stephen Lungu with you. Born in Harare, Zimbabwe, in 1942, Stephen was abandoned by his parents at the age of seven. With his brother and sister, Stephen spent the next few years being shifted from one home to the next, staying with relatives or living in orphanages. At the age of ten, to escape constant beatings, Stephen ran away from home and began living on the streets of Harare. He found shelter under a bridge which became his home for some years.

Longing to be loved and accepted, the ten-year-old Stephen welcomed the approaches of other street kids. However, their friendship lacked real love. They first introduced him to cigarettes, then to marijuana, then to glue sniffing and other drugs. Rummaging for food through bins in the white suburbs, Stephen was taught to take other necessities by knifepoint. The boy grew into a teenager and with his gang, the Black Shadows, robbed and stabbed his way to survival.

When he was about seventeen, Stephen and the Black Shadows joined the political struggle for the liberation of Zimbabwe. Stephen learned the skills of sabotage and terrorism, throwing petrol bombs and arranging riots. One Sunday after a political rally, the gang thought the moment was right to cause trouble. So, they decided to blow up a local bank. All twelve members filled their bags with petrol bombs and set out.

On route to their target Stephen and his gang came across a giant tent erected by the roadside. At first glance it looked like a circus and the guys thought it might be a good place to pick up girls. But peering inside they found it packed with thousands of people singing, praying and getting ready to hear a preacher talk about Jesus. Stephen's anger began to burn. The Black Shadows had strong feelings about the Bible. They believed it had been brought by westerners to brainwash black people. The whites, they felt, had used it to turn blacks into slaves while they took their land and gold and lived in riches. And having seen plenty of paintings of a Jesus with white skin, Stephen bitterly resented the idea of a "white man" being his God. When they discovered the tent's organisers were from the (then) apartheid-riddled South Africa, the gang's anger burned even more. They changed plans – and decided to blow the tent up instead. They would hurl their petrol bombs inside, then shoot those who tried to escape.

Stephen and the others first slipped into the tent to hear what was going on. An attractive young girl was on stage. This got Stephen's attention. She began sharing how she had been saved off the streets of Soweto by the love of God. Stephen felt a strange longing grow within him. The way the girl spoke, it seemed like she had discovered something truly wonderful. When the rest of the gang said it was time to start the raid, Stephen asked them to wait for just two more minutes while he listened further.

The girl finished and the preacher got up to read a verse from the Bible: "The wages of sin is death, but the gift of God is eternal life through Jesus Christ." The preacher then began his message – a passionate plea to get right with God, often spoken with tears. Stephen became confused. He had never heard anyone speak about God with such passion before.

"Though he was rich," the speaker said of Jesus' heavenly

origin, "for us he became poor." The preacher then described how Jesus, through his mysterious birth into the world, had been born in a dirty manger, how he'd been a refugee as a boy, had become a poor carpenter, and had later come to Jerusalem on a borrowed donkey, carried a borrowed cross, and been buried in a borrowed grave. He took on all this poverty, the speaker explained, so that we could enjoy his spiritual riches.

Stephen couldn't believe what he was hearing. This was a Jesus he could relate to, someone who knew what poverty was like.

As Stephen continued listening he felt like the preacher knew everything he'd done – the robbery, the violence, the hatred. Stephen turned to his friend and angrily accused him. "Why did you tell that man about *my* sins!" he yelled. The friend shouted back, "No, you told him about my sins!" They started fighting.

The next moment, Stephen broke down in tears. He picked up his weapons, walked towards the stage and knelt down. The preacher kept speaking for some time. Then the meeting was disturbed by a different gang and people started running for their lives. Forty minutes later, when the authorities had regained control, the preacher walked up to the humbled terrorist.

"Can your Jesus save a sinner like me?" Stephen asked him.

"Yes," the preacher replied. "God loves you."

The preacher opened his Bible to a Psalm and read: 'Though my father and mother forsake me, the Lord will receive me.' That verse was the final straw. Stephen fell back onto his knees. "God, please forgive me!" he cried out. "I'm tired of my lifestyle. Deliver me from my drug use." As he prayed, a deep peace flooded his heart. He felt clean.

He felt like the weight of his guilt had rolled off his shoulders.

Later that evening Stephen returned to the bridge he called home and knelt down once again. "God," he prayed, "you have saved me. Now I just want to tell the whole world about your love." While he was praying he sensed God's powerful Spirit touch his soul. Then he felt God speak to him:

Stephen, I will send you to nations you do not know. And I will open your eyes.

It's been many years since Stephen Lungu – an abandoned, illiterate, drug addicted terrorist – surrendered to God in a tent he was intending to blow up. And the promise given to him under that bridge has been proven true. Today Stephen speaks around the world about racial reconciliation, forgiveness and God's transforming love. He has addressed prime ministers, presidents and cabinet ministers in nations he once knew nothing of.

Stephen's eyes were opened to a new future once his past had been surrendered to God.[5]

Of all acts of man, repentance is the most divine. The greatest of all faults is to be conscious of none.

THOMAS CARLYLE

[surrendering to love]

We can read the drama of Stephen Lungu's story, or imagine the courageous abandon of Peter the fisherman, but we can still feel legitimate angst about surrendering to God ourselves. The relinquishment of our lives mustn't be done casually. Standing in the moment, considering the handover of future and past, we want to be sure. Whose hands are we leaping into? We've already discovered that God is powerful, creative and personal, the God found in the face of Jesus. But beyond that, who really is this deity and can he be trusted?

I have this feeling that in heaven we will learn something new about God every day, and yet forever be surprised. There will always be more to know. And yet, sacred Scripture, the Bible, is clear that out of the many words that can describe God, the greatest one to use is love. Love is his essential characteristic.[6]

Now, there's one aspect of God's loving nature I find so amazing that I struggle to express it with words. And it's this: God created us *after* he decided to rescue us.[7] God knew what was coming, he knew what we'd do, he knew the mess we'd get ourselves into and the abuse we'd throw at him. He could've ditched plans on life, the universe and everything. Yet out of love he went ahead and made us, after forming a plan to rescue us.

Just think about that for a while...

As God crafted the DNA string and designed the atom, drawing up matter's most basic elements; as he imagined earth and moon and sun and stars before each was created – as he did all this, God knew a greater problem would need his attention.

As God sketched dimensions on ozone layers and the mechanics of gravitational forces; as he dreamt of air and water, ice and mist; as he envisioned leaves and seeds, the shape of snowflakes and the felt-touch of petals – as God did all this, he considered the pain, and worked on a plan.

God dreamt up sound, volume, timbre and pitch. They'd be necessary for music, bird calls and dog barks, he decided. *Link sound to mass and shape,* I can hear God reflect, *and a bouncing ball will sound different from a falling tree. Focus some energy, make a beam of light, split that light into colours. Imagine the sunsets!* he exclaims.

What a shame it will all be ruined.

As God continued he imagined human beings. As he designed the complex eyeball, the nervous system, skeletal structures and tendons; as he shaped humanity's soul to love and work and create and laugh; as the excitement of breathing life into his beloved creatures almost overwhelmed him, God felt the heartbreak of those very creatures' betrayal. He foresaw the sin, the shame, the wickedness. He foresaw the world wars and genocides. He watched as greed and pride dehumanised his imagined humanity.

Is it worth it? I can imagine him wondering.

He glances back at his blueprints, the ones for the human hand. He considers the hand's function and design. And he imagines the day when the nails would plunge between the tendons of his own flesh.

Yes, it's worth it, he decides.

So he set the various worlds spinning, flung stars across the sky, cupped his hands to shape humanity and released them to run and sing. Heaven and earth knew no separation and the air bristled with life and excitement. All was bright, all was new, all lived well in a land so immersed in the radiance of God. Until the darkness came.

The shadows fell on the day of betrayal. The created tried to usurp the creator. Reaching for divinity, these small minds told the great mind his rules didn't matter. The singing stopped. The smiles fell. The followers turned their backs on the leader, sounding a deep thunderous note throughout the land.

It's all worth it, God says, wiping their spit from his eye.

Leaves began to droop, colours slightly faded, seasons became unstable. Sunsets lost their lustre and sounds lost their richness. Humanity's battle against itself, its earth and its God had begun. Fist met jaw, trust found treachery and the first tear fell. The ruin foreseen by God had come.

God took on the judge's role and the verdict was straightforward: humanity's evil would bring death, for life cannot flourish in darkness. But a greater word than death rested on heaven's heart. God would make a way for humanity to find life again – to find him again. He would bring redemption.

"It's not worth it," I can hear the enemy hiss; that venomous dark spirit of the ages.

This redemption would indeed be costly. Only objects of equal value could be traded. Only life can buy life. Only perfection can buy perfection. To bring back humanity's life and perfection a perfect life would have to be traded in their place.

"It's not worth it," the enemy spits, as the special moment in time comes and God glances down at the smoky, dusty streets of earth.

"It's not worth it!" the beast breathes anxiously, as Jesus prepares to enter our world, to live, feel and hurt like the rest of us.

"They're not worth it!" screams the fiend now, as Jesus clothes himself in the humanity of a baby born in a little Middle Eastern town.

And so this One, whom earth, sky and universe cannot contain, concentrated his greatness into the body of a boy. The boy became a man; the man began his mission – to find those who recognized they were lost and wanted to return to God.

Through miracle and wonder, compassion and power, his authority was revealed to those with open eyes. To the hopeless he shed meaning, to the bewildered he gave guidance, to the oppressed he brought liberation, to the forgotten he offered belonging. His deeds and words awakened something deep within those who watched and listened – a nostalgic longing for another world. A land under peaceful rule. A Kingdom like that lost so long ago.

Is it worth it? he prays in a lonely garden, as he looks down at his hands and contemplates the imminent event.

Again the creatures had turned. A friend, Judas, planted the kiss that ushered in the second great betrayal. The religious authorities called Jesus a blasphemer. The political authorities feared a revolt. Dodgy trial, whips and beatings. The hands of the made, flogged the body of the Maker.

It'll all be worth it, he gasps, carrying the bulky wooden cross up the hill.

The irony of it: God beneath his own creatures, their feet on his arms. Being pinned to two stumps of wood he had once caused to grow. Dust in his eyes from the earth he had formed. The original source of life now gradually fading.

"I told you," wheezes the dark spirit, sniggering.

"We told him," mutter the religious leaders, smugly.

"We failed him," cry his friends, having abandoned him for safety.

Crowds vied for a look, heavenly forces stood ready to intervene. Angels wept and demons convulsed as one, then the other arm stretched into place. A rusty nail, a heavy mallet, a bloody pierce through an exposed wrist. Another hit, and another. Another nail, and another for the feet. Lifted up, the cross shuddered into vertical position.

And the world was presented with its naked, bleeding, gasping God.

Then, the final breath.

Then cheering.

Weeping.

Darkness.

Daybreak, three days later. First Mary Magdalene. Then Peter the fisherman. Then a group of grief-stricken followers. He had appeared to them. Can it really be? They touched his wounds to prove it was him. Yes, yes it must be! He ate some food to prove he wasn't a ghost. It's him! He instructed, he forgave. He appeared to others, then he ascended to the sky.

The plan was complete.

Humanity's debt had been dealt with; betrayers' deaths traded for one life of perfection.

It was all worth it, I can hear him say.

Now, the lost can follow me home.

[the defining moment]

And so our hearts can settle a little. We are surrendering to a God of awesome power, but whose might and authority is channelled in love. As philosopher Blaise Pascal put it, "Jesus is the God whom we can approach without pride and before whom we can humble ourselves without despair."

A Chinese proverb says, "I dreamed a thousand new paths. I woke and walked my old one." There is risk in changing paths and surrendering to God (even a God of love) and humans are quite adept at allowing the inertia of tradition and the comfort of habit to keep us on old pathways. But through the ages a multitude has bent the knee and found it to be their defining moment. In fact, imagine how different history might be if some of those hadn't surrendered to God:

- Imagine if Mother Teresa had ignored that voice calling her to Calcutta's poor. How would history be different and who would she have become?

- Imagine if William Booth had left that Nottingham church early, and never founded the Salvation Army. Imagine a world without that legacy.

- Imagine if Handel had rejected the inspiration for his *Messiah*, Milton his *Paradise Lost*, Michelangelo his Sistine Chapel paintings.

- Imagine if Stephen Lungu had closed his heart, walked out of that tent, and reached into his bag of petrol bombs.

When our lives are complete we'll be able to look back and see three, four, maybe more, major turning points in our lives. Some will be common – marriage, career moves, perhaps migration to another country. Some may be unexpected – a crisis, a dream lost, the passing of a loved one. What God offers us in this moment of surrender is one of those defining moments – a turning point, a change of course, a decision that will make us the person God dreams of us becoming.

Imagine what your life could be when surrendered to God.

Imagine the history he may be waiting to write through you.

He who bears the sins of the world is fit to rule the world.

CHINESE PHILOSOPHER, LAO-TZE

The defining moments of my
life have not been my sins or
my successes. They've been
a depressingly small number
of decisions that involved
real risk.

AUTHOR, BRENNAN MANNING[8]

[open eyes]

It's been fifteen years since my own encounter with God. Looking back, I can see it has shaped my existence more than anything else. That surrender was my new beginning, my turning point, my rebirth into a life of miracle and adventure, guidance and belonging. I have not been spared life's difficulties and disappointments. I have experienced moments of doubt and confusion. And God still has some way to go in turning up the full luminescence of Christ within me, as I still fail him in little ways and large. Mine is not as dramatic a story as Stephen Lungu's, and my life is yet to leave the impact of Mother Teresa's. But in my own way I followed Peter the fisherman's lead, left everything, and followed Jesus. Since then my sense of purpose, vocation, geographic location, choice of life-partner and a myriad of life's other essentials have been given and directed by him. The joy has been immeasurable. Today, I can say with great certainty that nothing compares to the companionship of God.

We began this reflective journey in an arid wasteland, a desert with a secret. As scorching sun rose on the dry sand of that outback land each day, a giant river was found to flow just beneath its surface. For years eyes had not seen the reality that lay so near.

Similarly, today a thirsty generation is discovering there's more to life than dry materialism or the flattened world of secular thought. Something greater lies beyond the surface of life's existence.

Maybe some coincidences in life really aren't so coincidental.

Maybe some moments of serendipity are arranged just for us.

Maybe, just maybe, unseen footprints really do walk beside us.

Perhaps pain is a sign that we were never meant for a broken world like this. Perhaps yearnings are prompts of a God-shaped void, of a wholeness found in divine embrace. Perhaps God is whispering to us each day, a voice heard when listened for closely. Perhaps doubt can be a guide to God, a place where faith is actually strengthened. Perhaps the God of love can be encountered, surrendered to, and followed to a Kingdom of Light. And perhaps this God can put our often confused world back into perspective, and use us to make it better.

Perhaps the divine really can be encountered along life's path.

A God of love, with wounded wrists.

Follow me.

JESUS

>>> OTHER JOURNEY POINTS

Here are a few online destinations you may find helpful in exploring a life of divine companionship. In the majority of cases both the US and UK sites are listed, although most link to international sites as well. For matters regarding Christ and his way of life, the following are worth a look:

- **www.alpha.org** Groups meeting around the world to share a meal and talk about the meaning of life.

- **www.findachurch.com** (US) or **www.findachurch. co.uk** (UK) Connect with a faith community near you.

- **www.biblegateway.com** Read and listen to the world's most sold book (and the most shop-lifted book in the US. Go figure!).

- **www.comereason.org** Exploring some of the big questions of faith, doubt and belief. The Articles section is worth a browse.

- **www.rejesus.co.uk** Lots of voices and opinions on Christ and spirituality.

- **www.scriptureunion.gospelcom.net** Lots of helpful publications and courses for deepening the soul.

- **www.thethoughtfactory.net** I have to mention this one! A place to stimulate imagination, inspiration and spiritual growth. It's looked after by, um, me.

Some people have encountered God and then founded organisations that work at making this world a little like the world to come. So many groups could be mentioned here, so please take the list below as just a few worthy of support:

- **www.compassion.com** (US) or **www.compassionuk. org** (UK) Providing needy children around the world with food, clothing, education and a future.

- **www.habitat.org** Building homes for those needing shelter.

- **www.micahchallenge.org** A movement of individuals holding their governments to the United Nations' Millennium Development Goals of increasing aid, literacy and development for poor countries.

- **www.pfi.org** Prison Fellowship share God's love with the incarcerated, their families and their victims through social, spiritual and practical help.

- **www.tear.org.au** Working to support the relief and long-term development initiatives of poor communities around the world, with priority given to those most marginalised and exploited.

- **www.tearsoftheoppressed.org** A humanitarian group working for justice for those persecuted because of their beliefs.

- **www.teenchallenge.com** (US) or **www.teenchallenge. co.uk** (UK) A worldwide organisation with one of the highest success rates for teenage drug and alcohol rehabilitation.

- **www.worldvision.com** (US) or **www.wordvision.org. uk** (UK) Transforming lives by alleviating poverty and confronting its causes.

>>> SOURCES

TITLE PAGE Psalm chapter 77 verse 19, found in Jewish and Christian Scriptures.

CHAPTER 1 • PAIN: THE JOURNEY BEGINS

1 'Regeneration X: An Interview with Author Douglas Coupland', *Third Way*, May 1997.

CHAPTER 2 • YEARNING: THE JOURNEY INTENSIFIES

1 Reuters, March 8, 1999.

2 *Alive Magazine*, February, 1998.

3 'I'm on my own journey' interview by Cathleen Falsani, *Chicago Sun-Times*, August 8, 2004.

4 Charles Colson and Nancey Pearcey, *How Now Shall We Live?* London, Marshall Pickering, 1999, page 54.

5 CS Lewis, *Mere Christianity*, William Collins Sons and Co, Glasgow, 1952. page 128.

CHAPTER 3 • WHISPERS: THE JOURNEY'S SIGNPOSTS

1 TS Eliot, *Murder in the Cathedral*, quoted in David Tacey's *The Spirituality Revolution*, Harper Collins Publishers, Sydney, 2003, page 78

2 Found at www.gospelcom.net/lpea/firstpriority/summer2002/quotes.html.

3 A popularly revised wording of a phrase in Elizabeth Barrett Browning's book, *Aurora Leigh*, Bk. VII. 1, 1857, line 820.

4 Many of the following ideas have been sourced from Charles Colson and Nancy Pearcey's *How Now Shall We Live?*, London, Marshal Pickering, 2000, page 62-67. Other works worth pursuing on this theme include William Dembski's books *Intelligent Design: The Bridge Between Science and Theology*, Downer's Grove, Illinois, InterVarsity Press, 1999; *The Design Revolution: Answering the Toughest Questions About Intelligent Design*, Downer's Grove, Illinois, InterVarsity Press, 2004; and Michael J Behe's *Darwin's Black Box*, New York, Touchstone, 1996.

5 The blood clot and eyeball information here was taken from Professor Michael Behe's book *Darwin's Black Box*, New York, Touchstone, 1996. Behe quotes Charles Darwin's acknowledgement in *Origin of Species* that "If it could be demonstrated that any complex organ existed which could not possibly have been formed by numerous, successive, slight modifications, my theory would absolutely break down."

6 See the comments of Iowa State University astronomer Guillermo Gonzalez and Jay Richards from the Discovery Institute in the article Finding God in the Heavens by Rob Moll, www.christianitytoday.com/ct/2004/116/21.0.html

7 See Gregg Easterbrook's article The New Convergence in *Wired Magazine*, Issue 10.12, December 2002.

8 Allan Sandage, as mentioned in The New Convergence in *Wired Magazine*, Issue 10.12, December 2002.

9 Charles Towns, co-inventor of the laser, as mentioned in The New Convergence in *Wired Magazine*, Issue 10.12, December 2002.

10 Professor Anthony Flew made his thoughts public first in a letter to the August-September 2004 edition of Britain's *Philosophy Now* magazine and in December 2004 on a video titled *Has Science Discovered God?*

11 *The Twilight World of Bjork* by John Mulvey, August 11th, 2001.

12 Peter L. Berger, A *Rumour of Angels: Modern Society and the Rediscovery of the Supernatural*, Garden City, New York, Anchor Books, 1970.

13 This research was conducted by Harold G. Koenig of Duke University Medical Centre in North Carolina, United States and reported in "Spirituality May Help People Live Longer", CNN.com, November 17, 1999.

14 Research conducted by the Higher Education research Institute at the University of California-Los Angeles and reported in "Spiritually Inclined Students Happier" *USA Today*, November 4, 2004.

15 *Hardwired to Connect: The New Scientific Evidence for Authoritative Communities* report was conducted by the US-based Commission on Children at Risk (a joint initiative of the Dartmouth Medical School, the YMCA and the Institute for American Values) and reported on www.crosswalk.com/news/religiontoday/1309881.html

16 Interviewed in *Esquire* Magazine.

17 See the book of Genesis chapter 9, verses 8 to 16.

18 See Peter S Williams helpful article, "Aesthetic Arguments for the Existence of God", in the *Quodlibet Online Journal of Christian Theology and Philosophy,* Summer 2001, Vol. 3 n.3.

19 Evelyn Underhill, *Man and the Supernatural*, Methuen, 1934, page 170, as quoted in Peter S. Williams, "Aesthetic Arguments for the Existence of God", *Quodlibet Online Journal of Christian Theology and Philosophy,* Summer 2001, Vol. 3 n.3.

20 Anthony O'Hear, *After Progress*, Bloomsbury, 1999, as quoted in Peter S. Williams, "Aesthetic Arguments for the Existence of God", *Quodlibet Online Journal of Christian Theology and Philosophy*, Summer 2001, Vol. 3 n.3.

21 Philip Yancey, *Soul Survivor: How My Faith Survived the Church*, London, Hodder & Stoughton, 2001.

22 Personal interview with Philip Yancey, 2002.

23 See the New Testament book of Acts chapter 17, verse 27.

24 See the book of Acts chapter 14, verse 17.

25 Don Richardson, *Eternity In Their Hearts*, Ventura, California, Regal Books, revised edition,
1984, page 57.

26 'God's Talk' Me'en Style, *SIM NOW*, issue 80, page 2-3.

27 Personal radio interview with Dr. Michael Nazir-Ali, Bishop of Rochester, 2003.

28 There are a number of such courses around. Shona did Christianity Explained, a six-evening course that explores the basics of the faith. (www.christianityexplained.com)

29 This experience was shared during a church service at Redcliffe Christian Assembly in Queensland, Australia, Sunday 28 February, 1999.

30 The book of Psalms chapter 27, verse 8.

31 Johnny Lee Clary's website tells a little more of his story www.xkkk.org

CHAPTER 4 • ENCOUNTER: JOURNEY INTERRUPTED

1 *Seattle Times*, September 26th, 2002.

2 Donald Miller, *Searching For God Knows What*, Nashville, Tennessee, Thomas Nelson, 2004, page 21.

3 This concept is found in the twelfth chapter of the book of Matthew, verse 34.

4 JB Phillips, *Your God Is Too Small*, London, Epworth Press, 1966, page 70-71.

5 *The Lion, The Witch and The Wardrobe* is one of seven books in the Chronicles of Narnia series. Aslan's creation of Narnia is told in the first of the series, *The Magician's Nephew.*

6 CS Lewis, *The Lion the Witch and The Wardrobe*, London, Fontana Lions, 1950/1982, page 65.

7 CS Lewis, *Surprised by Joy*, Glasgow, Colins Fount, 1955/1987, page 182.

8 Colin Duriez, *A Field Guide To Narnia*, Downers Grove, Illinois, InterVarsity Press, 2004, page 46.

9 Bono in an interview with Cathleen Falsani of the Chicago Sun-Times.

10 I talk a little more about my parent's journey in a future book tentatively titled, *The Apprentice.*

11 *Juice Magazine*, Dec/Jan 2000/1.

12 The Ten Commandments are understood by Jews, Christians and others to be God's definitive guidelines for personal and community life. You can find them in the book of Exodus, chapter 20.

13 See the book of Deuteronomy, chapter 32, verse 39.

14 '[We] will all stand before God's judgement seat.' See the book of Romans chapter 14, verses 10 to 12.

15 Take a look at the book of Matthew chapter 25, verses 31 to 46.

16 CS Lewis, *The Lion, The Witch and The Wardrobe*, London, Fontana Lions, 1950/1982, page 166.

17 Read the beautiful Psalm 103.

18 See Psalms 139 and 45 as examples of this sentiment.

19 For example, Psalm 68 says that God is a "father to the fatherless" and "a defender of widows". The first chapter of the book of James says, "Religion that God our Father accepts as pure and faultless is this: to look after orphans and widows in their distress..."

20 The sixth chapter of Luke says that God is kind even to the "ungrateful and wicked," and the fourth chapter of 1 John says simply, "God is love."

21 "For God so loved the world that he gave his one and only Son, that whoever believes in him shall not perish but have eternal life." The book of John chapter 3, verse 16.

22 Richard J Foster, *Prayer*, London, Hodder and Stoughton, 1992, page 74.

CHAPTER 5 • DOUBT: THE JOURNEY'S CRISIS

1 David Tacey goes on to say, "Young people who tell the familiar story of dropping their religion are unaware of the secular myth in which they are held, and are unconscious of the new kind of conditioning that passes for personal liberation." David Tacey, *The Spirituality Revolution: the emergence of contemporary spirituality*, Sydney, Harper Collins, 2003, page 107-108.

2 *World*, July 28, 2001.

3 "Who Do You Worship?" Posted May, 2004, on news.bbc.co.uk/go/pr/fr/-/1/hi/talking_point/3477155.stm

4 *San Francisco* Examiner, June 23, 2003.

5 This promise is found in the Old Testament book of Jeremiah, chapter 29, verse 13.

6 This story of John The Baptist's doubt can be found in chapter 11 of the book of Matthew.

7 Thomas' experience can be read in the book of John, chapter 20, from verse 24.

8 Jesus was occasionally frustrated at his followers' lack of faith. Even after they had seen him perform numerous miracles they still doubted his ability to keep them safe (see the book of Mark, chapter 4), or that God would meet their needs for food and clothes (see the book of Matthew, chapter 6). It seems Thomas wasn't the only one to doubt Jesus' return from death, even though Jesus had told them that he would (see the book of Matthew, chapter 16).

9 CS Lewis, *Mere Christianity*, William Collins Sons and Co, Glasgow, 1952. page 121.

CHAPTER 6 • DREAM: TOWARDS A NEW WORLD

1 I have drawn this picture of heaven from biblical passages like chapters 21 and 22 of the book of Revelation, chapters 25 and 65 of the book of Isaiah (particularly verses 6 to 8 and 17 to 25 respectively) and chapter 5 of the book of Matthew.

2 Found in the second book of Corinthians, chapter 3 and verse 18, from *The Message* translation of the Bible.

3 What I have called the "Kingdom of Light" the Bible calls the "Kingdom of God" or the "Kingdom of Heaven". To read Jesus' words about the Kingdom having begun, take a look at the book of Matthew chapter 12, verses 22 to 28.

4 Frederick Buechner, *Wishful Thinking: A Theological ABC*, New York, Harper and Row, 1973.

5 Found in the book of James chapter 5, verses 13 to 16.

6 Sometimes God chooses not to miraculously heal us for our own benefit. I have written about this in an article called When God Doesn't Heal, originally published in *Discipleship Journal*, Issue 143, Sept/Oct 2004.

7 Found in the book of Romans, chapter 8, verses 9 to 11, quoted from *The Message* translation

of the Bible.

8   Found in the book of Mark, chapter 11, verse 24.

CHAPTER 7 • SURRENDER: SEEING THE DIVINE ALONG THE JOURNEY OF LIFE

1   I am indebted to Pete Greig for this story, which he tells in his book *The Vision and The Vow,* Florida, Relevant Books, 2004, page 17.

2   The book of Matthew, chapter 5, verse 8, from *The Message* translation of the Bible.

3   This story is found in the book of Luke, chapter 4, verse 38 and 39.

4   See the book of Luke, chapter 5.

5   This story was compiled from a personal interview with Stephen. His story has since been written in a book by Anne Coombs called *Out of the Black Shadows*, London, Monarch, 2001.

6   "God is love": the fourth chapter of 1 John.

7   If you want to check this out further, 1 Peter chapter 1 and verse 20 expresses the sentiment, and the thirteenth chapter of Revelation, verse 8.

8   Quoted in Pete Greig, *The Vision and The Vow*, Florida, Relevant Books, 2004, page 29.

>>> PHOTO ACKNOWLEDGEMENTS

All photographs have been taken by the Designer (Nicole Gillan) unless stated below:

Kodak	Natural images, page 7; desert, page 9; frond, page 23; beach trunks, page 45; water, cover sleeve.
Trista Weibell	Paw prints, page 11.
Craig May	(Model) page 13, also an invaluable photography assistant to the designer.
Photodisc	Hitchhiker, page 19; chains; page 97; traffic, page 45 and cover sleeve.
Susan Druitt	(Model) page 25.
PhotoInc*	Turtle, page 39 and back cover.
Neil Brooker	New Zealand slopes, page 51.
Ellen Mitchell	(Model) page 56; (Design Assistant) page 40.
Bobbie Osborne*	Rollercoaster, page 73.
Sheridan Voysey 112 ;	Rusty car, page 75; shadowy door, page 97; Cherborg posters, page Tasmanian piers, page 117; Isle of Wight trail, page 127
Peter Chen*	Stairs, page 75 and back cover.
Andrew Galpin	Wax over hand, page 78.
Clayton Hensen*	Lion, witch & wardrobe, page 88.
Nicholas Belton*	Sniffing, page 95.
Morguefile.com	Vents, page 97; garrison b, back cover.
Matthew Patrick	Chaos at the Brisbane RNA Show, page 98.
Tom Kerr	Sparkles, page 134.
R.Ramussen*	Guitarist, page 157.
Dainis Derics*	Working bees, page 144.
Scot Spencer*	Egg on the edge, page 166.

* found on istockphoto.com

>>> ABOUT THE AUTHOR

 Sheridan Voysey is a writer, speaker and broadcaster based in Sydney, Australia. He is the host of Open House, a live talkback show exploring life, faith and culture, heard on radio stations across Australis. Sheridan speaks regularly on issues of spirituality and belief, and is a featured columnist for *Alive Magazine*. He is married to Merryn, loves Thai food, is partial to dark chocolate, devours books, values solitude, hopes to one day own a puppy and is constantly working on his sense of humour.

For information on Sheridan's speaking schedule, or if you are interested in having Sheridan address your conference or group, visit his website: **www.thethoughtfactory.net.**